THE W

North Korea

Debra A. Miller, *Book Editor*

Daniel Leone, *President*
Bonnie Szumski, *Publisher*
Scott Barbour, *Managing Editor*

San Diego • Detroit • New York • San Francisco • Cleveland
New Haven, Conn. • Waterville, Maine • London • Munich

© 2004 by Greenhaven Press. Greenhaven Press is an imprint of The Gale Group, Inc., a division of Thomson Learning, Inc.

Greenhaven® and Thomson Learning™ are trademarks used herein under license.

For more information, contact
Greenhaven Press
27500 Drake Rd.
Farmington Hills, MI 48331-3535
Or you can visit our Internet site at http://www.gale.com

ALL RIGHTS RESERVED.
No part of this work covered by the copyright hereon may be reproduced or used in any form or by any means—graphic, electronic, or mechanical, including photocopying, recording, taping, Web distribution or information storage retrieval systems—without the written permission of the publisher.

Every effort has been made to trace the owners of copyrighted material.

Cover credit: © Reuters/Landov
National Archives, 10

Cover caption: Thousands of North Koreans take part in an anti-U.S. rally in Pyongyang on June 25, 2002, to mark the fifty-second anniversary of the invasion of South Korea.

LIBRARY OF CONGRESS CATALOGING-IN-PUBLICATION DATA

North Korea / Debra A. Miller, book editor.
    p. cm. — (The world's hot spots)
  Includes bibliographical references and index.
  ISBN 0-7377-2295-9 (pbk. : alk. paper) — ISBN 0-7377-2294-0 (lib. : alk. paper)
   1. Korea (North). 2. Nuclear weapons—Korea (North). I. Miller, Debra A. II. Series.
DS932.N64 2004
951.93—dc21
                                                           2003059903

Printed in the United States of America

CONTENTS

Foreword 7
Introduction 9

Chapter 1: The History of Tensions on the Korean Peninsula

1. **Japanese Rule and the Korean Independence Movement**
   by Bruce G. Cumings 17
   Japan annexed North Korea in 1919 and kept it as a Japanese colony until 1945. The colonial experience inspired resistance movements; it also produced leaders such as Kim Il Sung, who later became the president of North Korea.

2. **Korea Is Divided by Superpower Occupation and War**
   by Han Woo-keun 21
   When Japan was ousted from Korea at the end of World War II, Koreans looked forward to independence. Instead, however, Korea was divided and occupied by the Soviet Union and the United States, creating two separate nations and leading to a civil Korean War.

3. **Kim Il Sung Continues Attacks on South Korea**
   by Guy R. Arrigoni 32
   Tension between North and South Korea grew throughout the 1960s, 1970s, and 1980s, as North Korean leader Kim Il Sung orchestrated military infiltrations, guerrilla attacks, and assassination attempts against South Korean leaders as part of a strategy to reunite the two Koreas.

4. **North Korea's Famine and Economic Crisis**
   by Don Oberdorfer 35
   In the 1990s North Korea experienced an economic crisis caused by the collapse of the Soviet Union, followed by floods and droughts that resulted in a severe famine and mass starvation.

Chapter 2: North Korea and Weapons of Mass Destruction

1. North Korea Is a Terrorist State
by George W. Bush   45
Korea is one of several nations that possess or seek to obtain weapons of mass destruction and pose a terrorist threat to the world.

2. North Korea Has Nuclear, Chemical, and Biological Weapons and Missiles to Deliver Them
by John Bolton   50
The United States is gravely concerned about North Korea's continuing development of weapons of mass destruction and its sale of ballistic missiles and missile technology.

3. North Korea's New Nuclear Weapons Threats: Crisis and Opportunity
by James T. Laney and Jason T. Shaplen   57
North Korea's admission that it is again developing nuclear weapons has created both a new international crisis and an opportunity for the United States and the regional powers to negotiate a solution to the North Korean problem.

4. U.S. Policy Toward North Korea Is Vicious and Hostile
by the Democratic People's Republic of Korea   68
North Korea justifies its withdrawal from the Nuclear Non-Proliferation Treaty by claiming that U.S. policy is vicious and hostile.

5. North Korea Poses a Major Nuclear Threat
by Lou Dobbs   72
The threat of North Korean leader Kim Jong Il and the country's nuclear weapons program could have a devastating global effect. North Korea could soon have enough nuclear material to build five or six nuclear bombs.

6. U.S. Policy Must Respond to North Korea's Intentions
by Phillip C. Saunders   75
In order to choose the right approach in its negotiations with North Korea, the United States must discover North Korea's hidden intentions.

7. Negotiation with North Korea Is Doomed to Failure
by Bok Ku Lee   85
A North Korean defector describes why he believes the United States should not agree to give any assistance to North Korea in exchange for its agreements to stop its weapons of mass destruction programs.

Chapter 3: North Korean Instability and the Asian-Pacific Region

1. North Korea's Weapons of Mass Destruction Threaten South Korea
by Bruce Bennett   90
North Korea's new military strategy is to use weapons of mass destruction to catastrophically damage South Korean and U.S. forces to the point where outdated North Korean conventional equipment and weapons might still be effective.

2. A Nuclear North Korea Could Lead to an Arms Race in Asia
by Thomas Omestad et al.   94
U.S. policy makers' worst fear is that a nuclear North Korea could lead to a new arms race in Asia, in which Japan decides to go nuclear, followed by South Korea and other smaller countries. In turn, China and Russia could respond by increasing their existing nuclear and missile programs.

3. North Korean Actions Could Cause Japan to Reconsider Pacifism
by Alex Kerr   98
North Korea's menacing actions, including its firing of a missile over Japan in 1998 and its nuclear weapons programs, have caused some leaders in Japan to consider

acquiring nuclear weapons and missiles and taking military action against North Korea.

4. China Seeks Reform of North Korea
by David Shambaugh 101
China's priorities for its North Korean policy includes regime reform, a phased integration of North and South Korea, normalization of relations between North Korea and the United States, and a containment of North Korea's nuclear program.

Chronology 111
For Further Research 120
Index 124

FOREWORD

The American Heritage Dictionary defines the term *hot spot* as "an area in which there is dangerous unrest or hostile action." Though it is probably true that almost any conceivable "area" contains potentially "dangerous unrest or hostile action," there are certain countries in the world especially susceptible to conflict that threatens the lives of noncombatants on a regular basis. After the events of September 11, 2001, the consequences of this particular kind of conflict and the importance of the countries, regions, or groups that produce it are even more relevant for all concerned public policy makers, citizens, and students. Perhaps now more than ever, the violence and instability that engulfs the world's hot spots truly has a global reach and demands the attention of the entire international community.

The scope of problems caused by regional conflicts is evident in the extent to which international policy makers have begun to assert themselves in efforts to reduce the tension and violence that threatens innocent lives around the globe. The U.S. Congress, for example, recently addressed the issue of economic stability in Pakistan by considering a trading bill to encourage growth in the Pakistani textile industry. The efforts of some congresspeople to improve the economic conditions in Pakistan through trade with the United States was more than an effort to address a potential economic cause of the instability engulfing Pakistani society. It was also an acknowledgment that domestic issues in Pakistan are connected to domestic political issues in the United States. Without a concerted effort by policy makers in the United States, or any other country for that matter, it is quite possible that the violence and instability that shatters the lives of Pakistanis will not only continue, but will also worsen and threaten the stability and prosperity of other regions.

Recent international efforts to reach a peaceful settlement of the Israeli-Palestinian conflict also demonstrate how peace and stability in the Middle East is not just a regional issue. The toll on Palestinian and Israeli lives is easy to see through the suicide bombings and rocket attacks in Israeli cities and in the occupied territories of the West Bank and Gaza. What is, perhaps, not as evident is the extent to which this conflict involves the rest of the world. Saudi Arabia and Iran, for instance, have long been at odds and have attempted to gain control of the conflict by supporting competing organizations dedicated to a

Palestinian state. These groups have often used Saudi and Iranian financial and political support to carry out violent attacks against Israeli civilians and military installations. Of course, the issue goes far beyond a struggle between two regional powers to gain control of the region's most visible issue. Many analysts and leaders have also argued that the West's military and political support of Israel is one of the leading factors that motivated al-Qaeda's September 11 attacks on New York and Washington, D.C. In many ways, this regional conflict is an international affair that will require international solutions.

The World's Hot Spots series is intended to meet the demand for information and discussion among young adults and students who would like to better understand the areas embroiled in conflicts that contribute to catastrophic events like those of September 11. Each volume of The World's Hot Spots is an anthology of primary and secondary documents that provides historical background to the conflict, or conflicts, under examination. The books also provide students with a wide range of opinions from world leaders, activists, and professional writers concerning the root causes and potential solutions to the problems facing the countries covered in this series. In addition, extensive research tools such as an annotated table of contents, bibliography, and glossaries of terms and important figures provide readers a foundation from which they can build their knowledge of some of the world's most pressing issues. The information and opinions presented in The World's Hot Spots series will give students some of the tools they will need to become active participants in the ongoing dialogue concerning the globe's most volatile regions.

🔥 INTRODUCTION

North Korea is high on the list of countries that U.S. policy makers view as possible "rogue" nations that pose a threat to their neighbors and the world. U.S. president George W. Bush, for example, claimed in early 2002 that the regime of Kim Jong Il in North Korea is part of an "axis of evil," along with Iraq and Iran, which threatens the peace of the world by supporting terror and developing weapons of mass destruction. North Korea appeared to confirm this characterization when, in October 2002, it admitted to U.S. negotiators that it had been secretly developing a uranium-enrichment nuclear weapons program, contrary to the terms of a 1994 agreement with the United States stating North Korea would not seek nuclear weapons.

However, North Korea's motives are far from clear. Since the 1991 collapse of the Soviet Union, its main supporter, North Korea has faced a devastating decline in its economy and a loss of national security, and many experts believe that it seeks nuclear and other weapons both as a negotiating tool to acquire economic aid and for its national defense. Whether North Korea's intentions are truly evil, or whether it is merely seeking to survive and defend itself, is difficult to discern.

Indeed, North Korea's 2002 announcement renewed the debate in the international community about how best to deal with North Korea—a small, volatile Communist country that has survived, despite its severe economic problems, long after most Communist governments in the world have collapsed. Created in 1948 with a Soviet-style government, North Korea has developed as a typical Communist-bloc country, with an economy planned and controlled by the state, an absolute leader who modeled himself after Soviet dictator Joseph Stalin, a strong military, and a foreign policy antagonistic toward South Korea and other countries affiliated with the West. North Korea's 2002 threat to develop nuclear weapons is only the latest in a long series of military threats made by the small country in the half-century since its formation.

North Korea's Search for Korean Unity

At the heart of North Korea's militaristic policies is a strong drive for Korean unification and independence, developed through a long history of foreign occupation and influence on the Korean peninsula. Although ancient Korea successfully fought invaders and prospered for five centuries as a unified and independent kingdom under the Choson dynasty (1392–1910), imperial Japan brutally colonized the Korean peninsula in 1910 and held it for almost four decades. The Japanese imposed military rule, confiscated Korean land, and sought to eliminate Korean culture, creating a deep resentment among Koreans who were subjected to Japanese rule. The colonial period only fueled the Koreans' strong desire for independence and unity. It also inspired nationalist and Communist resistance movements opposed to Japanese rule. Indeed, the leaders of the anti-Japanese independence movement eventually became the leaders of North Korea and South Korea; one branch of anti-Japanese Communist guerrilla fighters, for example, formed the regime headed by Kim Il Sung that still governs North Korea today through Kim's son, Kim Jong Il.

Modern North Korea's dedication to Korean unification and independence was further fueled by the U.S. and Soviet occupation of the Korean peninsula following World War II. Although the two World

Thousands of North Korean refugees flee Hungnam during the military evacuation in December 1950.

War II allies liberated Korea from Japanese rule, Koreans' burning desire for a unified, independent Korea after the Japanese occupation was frustrated by these new foreign occupiers. From 1945 to 1948 Korea was subjected to a military occupation; in 1948 the peninsula was formally divided into two separate countries, North and South Korea. Koreans' frustration over the country's division ultimately led to the Korean War, ignited in June 1950 when North Korea attacked South Korea in an attempt to force the South to unify with the North under Communist rule. However, the war failed to unify Korea. The United States entered the war to defend South Korea while the Soviets and Chinese backed North Korea, making the conflict to some extent a proxy war between international superpowers and leading eventually to a stalemate and truce in 1953 between North and South Korea.

After the war, North Korean leader Kim Il Sung built up his military and pursued a campaign of hostilities toward South Korea and its ally, the United States, that continues to the present day. During the 1960s and 1970s, for example, North Korea waged a guerrilla war against South Korea that included attacks on ships and aircraft, military raids, and attempted assassinations. Later, Kim Il Sung shifted to more of a terrorist strategy, emphasizing civilian over military targets. For example, in 1983, North Korea attacked South Korean president Chun Doo Hwan by bombing a South Korean cabinet meeting in Rangoon, Burma; the explosion did not harm Chun Doo Hwan but did kill seventeen Koreans and four Burmese. In November 1987 a North Korean agent bombed a (South) Korean Air commercial aircraft, killing all 115 people aboard and earning North Korea a place on the U.S. list of countries that practice terrorism.

Since the 1980s, North Korea has sought to add nuclear weapons and other weapons of mass destruction to its military arsenal. This led to an international crisis in 1993, when North Korea refused to allow international inspections of its nuclear facilities after evidence indicated weapons development was under way in violation of treaties it had signed. Talks with the United States defused the crisis and resulted in the 1994 Framework Agreement, under which North Korea agreed to freeze its nuclear weapons programs in exchange for fuel oil and aid in building light water reactors for electrical production.

North Korea in Crisis

Since the early 1990s North Korea has faced mounting threats to its very survival. The collapse of the Soviet Union in 1991 and China's embrace of capitalist economic policies left North Korea without the economic support and military protection of its traditional Communist allies. In 1995–1996 North Korea was hit by flooding and drought that destroyed

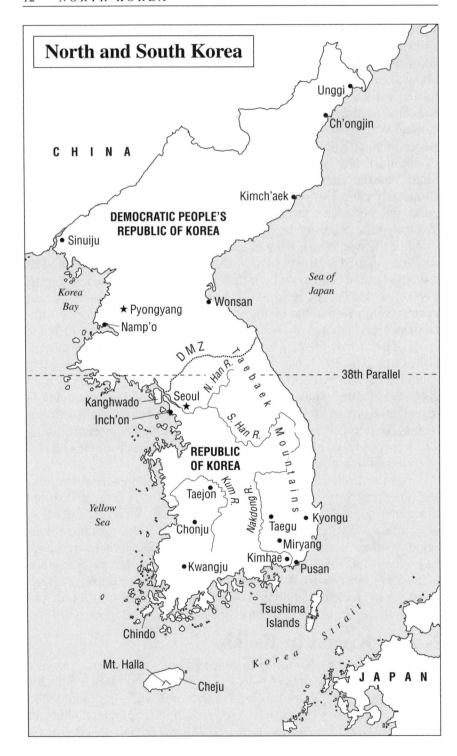

agricultural harvests and cropland. Unable to rely on its Communist allies for food aid, North Korea soon suffered a devastating famine that brought malnutrition and starvation to hundreds of thousands of its people. The loss of the Communist-bloc aid and trade also threw North Korea's economy into a downward spiral, and by the end of the 1990s many observers predicted North Korea was on the verge of collapse.

Analysts underestimated the resilience of the Communist government in North Korea, however. North Korea requested food aid from the United Nations and allowed some limited economic reform—enough to pull the country through the worst of the food famine, albeit with much suffering and many deaths. Then, instead of fully embracing foreign assistance and interaction that might have stabilized the country economically, the North Korean government, now headed by Kim Jong Il (Kim Il Sung's son and successor), receded into greater isolation and opted to further strengthen its military, largely by pursuing nuclear weapons, other weapons of mass destruction, and missile development. North Korea also stepped up arms dealing, selling missiles and missile technology for cash to prop up its ailing economy, creating further international concerns. Throughout these troubles, and despite certain diplomatic overtures to South Korea which at first appeared promising, North Korea maintained its fierce posture toward the West and continued its provocative actions toward South Korea, the United States, and other pro-Western countries such as Japan.

In the late 1990s South Korea and the United States adopted policies of engagement and negotiation aimed at forging a peaceful relationship with North Korea that could eventually lead to reunification with the South. These policies were based on a belief that North Korea's actions were increasingly motivated by security and economic survival fears caused by the lack of Communist military and economic support. Although these efforts produced some diplomatic successes, such as the 1994 Framework Agreement between North Korea and the United States and a summit between North and South Korea in 2000 that helped reunite Korean families separated by the war, North Korea did not curb its military activities. Indeed, in 1998 it launched a medium-range missile over the Sea of Japan, demonstrating its possession of longer-range missiles and its ability to attack not only South Korea and U.S. forces stationed there, but also Japan. The United States also suspected that North Korea again had begun secretly developing nuclear weapons, in violation of its 1994 agreement.

North Korea's Threat

The first decade of the twenty-first century brought only more uncertainty about North Korea's intentions and future. After President

George W. Bush took office in January 2001, he directed a review of U.S. policy toward North Korea. Its recommendations included continuing diplomatic efforts, but events soon changed the Bush administration's approach. First, on September 11, 2001, terrorists launched catastrophic attacks on U.S. soil in New York and Washington, D.C. President Bush responded to the attacks by declaring a "war on terror," noting that this war would target not only terrorist organizations but also countries that harbor or sponsor terrorism. Later, after the United States successfully toppled the Taliban regime in Afghanistan that had provided sanctuary to al-Qaeda terrorists, Bush gave a State of the Union address in which he named three other states that sponsor terrorism and seek weapons of mass destruction—Iraq, Iran, and North Korea. This speech suggested a shift in U.S. policy away from a primarily defensive posture toward preemptive strikes that remove potential security threats to the United States. This change in U.S. policy clearly could affect North Korea, especially since the United States has set a precedent by attacking Iraq, one of the other two countries cited as dangerous by Bush.

When representatives of the Bush administration and North Korean negotiators finally met in October 2002, North Korea unexpectedly confirmed U.S. suspicions that it was again developing nuclear weapons. The North even suggested that it possessed other powerful weapons, a comment that the United States interpreted as referring to chemical and biological weapons. North Korea proposed a nonaggression treaty with the United States to end the crisis. The United States, distracted by its preparations for its war to overthrow the Iraqi regime of Saddam Hussein and seeking to involve North Korea's Asian neighbors, proposed multinational negotiations, while North Korea continued to demand bilateral talks with only the United States. Meanwhile, North Korea, in typical fashion, escalated tensions by provocative actions that included evicting international inspectors, activating nuclear reactors that it had shut down in 1994, and pulling out of the Nuclear Non-Proliferation Treaty, the principal arms control treaty among the international community. Ultimately, talks began in April 2003 between North Korea, the United States, and China, but as of the fall of 2003, the crisis had not been resolved.

The threat posed by a nuclear North Korea is clear to U.S. policy makers. North Korea is believed to possess two nuclear bombs already, as well as missiles that can reach not only South Korea and Japan, but also the continental United States. U.S. intelligence also is certain that North Korea has chemical and biological weapons in large quantities. If North Korea pursues its nuclear weapons program, it could theoretically produce many nuclear weapons in a relatively short period of time, raising the possibility that it might use these weapons offensively. Perhaps even worse, North Korea could sell the weapons to other rogue countries or terrorists in exchange for cash to prop up its deteriorating economy.

In addition, North Korea's neighbors fear that a nuclear North Korea could provoke a nuclear arms race in Asia, if countries such as South Korea and Japan feel compelled to acquire nuclear weapons and missiles to deter nuclear attacks by the North. Such a development could derail the positive and cooperative economic relationships that have developed in recent decades among Asian countries such as South Korea, China, and Japan. North Korea's instability, both military and economic, also threatens the peace process that has begun between the two Koreas and efforts toward a peaceful reunification of the Korean peninsula. Indeed, even if the 2002–2003 nuclear weapons crisis is resolved, South Korea fears an economic collapse in North Korea could cost the South many billions of dollars if the South suddenly has to provide economic and humanitarian aid.

The dilemma facing policy makers today is determining the true intentions of the North Korean regime. Is it a dangerous rogue state still intent on reunifying with South Korea by force and bent on missile and other arms proliferation? Or are North Korea's provocative actions motivated by fears about its survival, and calculated to acquire aid and security by forcing negotiation? Answering these questions is an exceedingly difficult task.

The ultimate outcome of the 2002 nuclear crisis, therefore, and the fate of North Korea remains uncertain at this time. However, North Korea may be facing a new set of challenges from the United States, which twice since September 11, 2001, has attacked regimes believed to be dangerous to U.S. and world security. The United States already considers North Korea a dangerous rogue state. Whether the United States, together with other Asian countries such as China, can restrain the North Korean threat of weapons of mass destruction and stabilize the country economically without resorting to military action, and how North Korea might respond to any such initiatives, has yet to be resolved.

CHAPTER 1

The History of Tensions on the Korean Peninsula

Japanese Rule and the Korean Independence Movement

By Bruce G. Cumings

After five centuries of Korean independence and unity under the Choson dynasty, imperial Japan annexed Korea as a colony in 1910. The Japanese did not leave until 1945, after being defeated by the Allies in World War II. The colonial experience for Korea during this period was a bitter one, characterized by great humiliation for Koreans and hatred of the Japanese rulers. However, the Japanese occupation also modernized the Korean economy and society.

As this selection, written by Bruce G. Cumings for the Library of Congress, explains, the colonial period shaped the leadership of post-1945 Korea. Cumings describes how nationalist and Communist resistance movements arose to fight the Japanese occupation and how leaders of these movements eventually became the leaders of North and South Korea after the country was divided following World War II. For example, North Korean leader Kim Il Sung had been part of the Communist resistance movement in the 1930s in Manchuria and was viewed by the Japanese as one of the most effective and dangerous guerrilla fighters. North Korea, therefore, traces its leadership and ideology back to this Japanese resistance.

Bruce G. Cumings is a professor of East Asian and international history at the University of Chicago.

Bruce G. Cumings, "Historical Setting," *North Korea: A Country Study*, edited by Andrea Matles Savada. Washington, DC: Library of Congress, 1994.

In 1910 Japan turned Korea into its colony, thus extinguishing Korea's hard-fought independence, which had first emerged [during the period of 108 B.C. to A.D. 313].

Collapse of Unified Korean Rule

Under Japanese imperial pressure that began in earnest with Korea's opening in 1876, the [Korean] Chosŏn Dynasty faltered and then collapsed in a few decades. The dynasty had had an extraordinary five-century longevity, but although the traditional system could adapt to the changes necessary to forestall or accommodate domestic or internal conflict and change, it could not withstand the onslaught of technically advanced imperial powers with strong armies. The old agrarian bureaucracy had managed the interplay of different and competing interests by having a system of checks and balances that tended over time to equilibrate the interests of different parties. The king and the bureaucracy kept watch over each other, the royal clans watched both, scholars criticized or remonstrated from the moral position of Confucian doctrine, secret inspectors and censors went around the country to watch for rebellion and ensure accurate reporting, landed aristocrats sent sons into the bureaucracy to protect family interests, and local potentates influenced the county magistrates sent down from the central administration. The Chosŏn Dynasty was not a system that modern Koreans would wish to restore, but it was a sophisticated political system, adaptable enough and persistent enough to have given unified rule to Korea for half a millennium.

The Legacy of Japanese Colonialism

Korea did not escape the Japanese grip until 1945, when Japan lay prostrate under the Allied victory that brought World War II to a close. The colonial experience that shaped postwar Korea was intense and bitter. It brought development and underdevelopment, agrarian growth and deepened tenancy, industrialization and extraordinary dislocation, and political mobilization and deactivation. It also spawned a new role for the central state, new sets of Korean political leaders, communism and nationalism, and armed resistance and treacherous collaboration. Above all, it left deep fissures and conflicts that have gnawed at the Korean national identity ever since.

Colonialism was often thought to have created new countries where none existed before, drawn national boundaries, brought diverse tribes and peoples together, tutored the natives in self-government, and prepared for the day when the colonialist power decided to grant independence. But all this had existed in Korea for centuries before 1910. Furthermore, by virtue of their relative proximity to China, Koreans had always felt superior to Japan and blamed Japan's devastating sixteenth-century invasions for hindering Korean wealth and power in subsequent centuries.

Thus the Japanese engaged not in creation but in substitution after 1910: substituting a Japanese ruling elite for the Korean . . . scholar-officials, colonial imperative coordination for the old central state administration, Japanese modern education for Confucian classics, Japanese capital and expertise for the budding Korean versions, Japanese talent for Korean talent, and eventually the Japanese language for Korean. Koreans never thanked the Japanese for these substitutions, did not credit Japan with creations, and instead saw Japan as snatching away the ancient regime, Korea's sovereignty and independence, its indigenous if incipient modernization, and above all its national dignity. Koreans never saw Japanese rule as anything but illegitimate and humiliating. Furthermore, the very closeness of the two nations—in geography, in common Chinese cultural influences, and in levels of development until the nineteenth century—made Japanese dominance all the more galling to Koreans and gave a peculiar intensity to their love/hate relationship. . . .

The Rise of Korean Nationalism and Communism

The colonial period brought forth an entirely new set of Korean political leaders, spawned by both the resistance to and the opportunities of Japanese colonialism. In 1919 mass movements swept many colonial and semicolonial countries, including Korea. Drawing on [U.S. president] Woodrow Wilson's promises of self-determination, on March 1, 1919, a group of thirty-three intellectuals petitioned for independence from Japan and touched off nationwide mass protests [later known as the "March First Movement"] that continued for months. These protests were put down fiercely by the Japanese, causing many younger Koreans to become militant opponents of colonial rule. The year was a watershed for imperialism in Korea: the leaders of the movement, predominantly Christian and Western in outlook, were moderate intellectuals and students who sought independence through nonviolent means and support from progressive elements in the West. Their courageous witness and the nationwide demonstrations that they provoked remained a touchstone of Korean nationalism. The movement succeeded in provoking reforms in Japanese administration, but its failure to realize independence also stimulated radical forms of anticolonial resistance. In the 1930s, new groups of armed resisters, bureaucrats, and—for the first time—military leaders emerged. Both North Korea and South Korea were profoundly influenced by the political elites and the political conflicts generated during colonial rule. . . .

Guerrilla Resistance and North Korea

Some Korean militants went into exile in China and the Soviet Union and founded early communist and nationalist resistance groups. The Korean Communist Party (KCP) was founded in Seoul in 1925; one of the organizers was Pak Hŏn-yŏng, who became the leader of Korean communism in southern Korea after 1945. Various nationalist groups also emerged during this period, including the exiled Korean Provisional Government (KPG) in Shanghai, which included Syngman Rhee and another famous nationalist, Kim Ku, among its members.

Police repression and internal factionalism made it impossible for radical groups to exist for any length of time. Many nationalist and communist leaders were jailed in the early 1930s. . . . When Japan invaded and then annexed Manchuria in 1931, however, a strong guerrilla resistance embracing both Chinese and Koreans emerged. There were well over 200,000 guerrillas—all loosely connected and including bandits and secret societies—fighting the Japanese in the early 1930s; after murderous but effective counterinsurgency campaigns, the numbers declined to a few thousand by the mid-1930s. It was from this milieu that Kim Il Sung [later the leader of North Korea] . . . emerged. By the mid-1930s, he had become a significant guerrilla leader whom the Japanese considered one of the most effective and dangerous of guerrillas. They formed a special counterinsurgent unit to track Kim down, and they put Koreans in it as part of their divide-and-rule tactics.

Both Koreas have spawned myths about the guerilla resistance: North Korea claims that Kim single-handedly defeated the Japanese, and South Korea claims that the present-day ruler of North Korea is an impostor who stole the name of a revered patriot. Nonetheless, the resistance is important for understanding postwar Korea. Resistance to Japan became the main legitimating doctrine of North Korea: North Koreans trace the origin of their army, leadership, and ideology back to this resistance. For the next five decades, the top North Korean leadership was dominated by a core group that had fought the Japanese in Manchuria.

Korea Is Divided by Superpower Occupation and War

By Han Woo-keun

After the 1945 defeat of Japan by the Allies in World War II, Japanese rule over Korea ended and Koreans believed independence was at hand. However, as explained in the following excerpt by Han Woo-keun, a professor of history in South Korea, the nation instead was occupied by the Soviet Union and the United States. Although the two superpowers made efforts to form a trusteeship that would promote Korean unification and independence, the Soviet-American relationship deteriorated into a Cold War standoff. As a result, each power followed a policy of nurturing its own style of government in the area it controlled. This led to the creation of a Communist government in North Korea under the leadership of Kim Il Sung and the development of a democratic-style government in South Korea.

Nevertheless, Koreans continued to seek unification and independence. Following the May 1948 elections in South Korea, a popular organization promoting unification, the Democratic Front for the Unification of the Fatherland, was founded by leaders of both North and South Korea to create a new, unified Korean government. However, this effort was thwarted when the South Korean government rejected the overtures. The North Korean government then presented a plan for reunification to the South Korean national assembly, which was also rejected. Shortly thereafter, North Korea abandoned its efforts for peaceful reunification and invaded South Korea, starting the Korean War in 1950.

Han Woo-keun, *The History of Korea*. Seoul, Korea: The Eul-Yoo Publishing Company, 1970. Copyright © 1970 by Han Woo-keun. Reproduced by permission of the publisher.

While intensifying her oppression of Korea, Japan was beginning the series of military conquests that brought her into World War II and finally resulted in her defeat and Korea's liberation. Deliberate military provocation [by the Japanese] in Manchuria in 1931 resulted in the setting up in the following year of the puppet kingdom of "Manchukuo" under Japanese rule and also in placing the leading militarists in complete control of the Japanese government. Clashes with China increased until a state of all-out war was reached in 1937. Taking advantage of the preoccupation of the Western powers with the threat of war in Europe, Japan began to move into Southeast Asia, and when France fell in 1940 occupied French Indochina and Siam, threatening British positions in Burma and Malaya. Then began the farce of the "Greater East Asia Co-Prosperity Sphere," with Japan posing as the liberator of the Asian peoples from Western colonialism while treating those she conquered just as badly and sometimes worse than ever the Westerners had. The nationalist movements that were about to break out on every land in Asia were ignored or suppressed.

In 1940 Japan took another step toward world war by concluding a military alliance with Germany and Italy. At the end of 1941, frustrated in her attempts to obtain American sanction for her conquests and angered by the United States' refusal to continue supplying her with war materials, Japan took the fateful step of provoking war by the attack on Pearl Harbor, Hawaii, December 7, 1941. The United States Navy was badly hurt, and at first Japan swept all before her. In 1942 the Americans were driven out of the Philippines and the British strongholds of Hong Kong and Singapore fell. Japanese troops fanned out to northern New Guinea and most of the adjacent smaller islands and took the strategic American base on Guam. There seemed no stopping them.

But the turning point had already come, with the battle of Midway Island, in June 1942, from which a severely mauled Japanese navy limped home in secrecy. Japanese expansion in the Pacific was stopped at that point, and in the following year the tide began to turn. One by one, the conquered islands were retaken and the Japanese forces pushed back. Meanwhile, the dictator [Benito] Mussolini was overthrown in Europe and Italy surrendered to the Allies. With prospects of victory good in both theaters of war, the leaders of the United States, Great Britain and China met at Cairo at the end of November 1943, to confer on strategy and post-war policy. In the Cairo Declaration which embodied the results of this conference, they announced that the war would continue until Japan surrendered unconditionally, that all Japanese territory acquired since 1894 should be returned to its previous owners, and that Korea should in due time become a free and independent nation.

In 1944 came the [Allied] invasion of Normandy, opening the last chapter of Hitler's mad career in Europe. Germany surrendered in May of 1945, and the Allied Powers turned their full attention to Asia. On July 26 the leaders of the United States, Great Britain, the Soviet Union and China met at Potsdam and issued the Potsdam Declaration, again demanding the unconditional surrender of Japan. The Japanese, determined to struggle to the bitter end, refused. On August 6 the first atomic bomb obliterated Hiroshima, and on August 9 another fell on Nagasaki. Russia declared war on Japan on August 9, and within five days was in full control of northeastern Manchuria and northern Korea. Japan finally surrendered on August 15.

Koreans Oppressed by the Japanese

The war in the Pacific involved great suffering for Korea, especially in its later stages, for as Japan's defeat drew nearer her exactions and oppressions increased. Korea began being used as a supply base with the outbreak of war with China in 1937. In addition, as Japanese rice production fell because of a manpower shortage, more and more Korean rice went to Japan. Between 1917 and 1938 Korean rice exports rose tenfold, finally reaching over fifty million bushels. In addition, cattle were confiscated for meat and metal objects of all kinds, including scrap iron, brass pots and dishes, and even metal spoons and chopsticks were seized for the munitions factories. Japanese soldiers were everywhere. There were 46,000 of them in 1941 and 59,000 in 1943. By 1944 they had increased to 68,000, and in the disastrous year of 1945 the number leaped to 300,000.

A Japanese general, Minami Jiro, was appointed Governor-General in 1936. In 1937 the notorious "assimilation" policy was put into effect. Henceforth all educational institutions were to use the Japanese language exclusively. In 1940 the leading Korean-language newspapers were suppressed and in 1942 the last two literary magazines in Korean disappeared. In October of 1942 most of the members of the Korean Language Society were arrested and imprisoned on the pretext that they were secretly fomenting a nationalistic movement against Japanese rule. Scholarly and literary groups were dissolved.

From then on, all meetings and ceremonies in Korea began with an oath of allegiance to the Japanese Emperor, and Koreans were compelled to worship at Japanese Shinto shrines. In 1939 the assimilation movement reached a height of absurdity when all Koreans were ordered to change their names to Japanese ones.

As the war extended, Japan ran short of manpower and Korea was forced to supply the need. In 1938 a "volunteer" system, which was anything but voluntary, began conscripting Korean youths. In 1939 the

Japanese began using forced Korean labor in mines and factories and military construction abroad. By the end of the war 2,616,900 persons were engaged in forced labor in Korea, while 723,900 had been sent abroad. Japanese patriotic societies were set up and Koreans forced to join them. In 1942 Korean men began being drafted into the Japanese army. As the strain on Japanese resources reached the breaking point and defeat loomed over her, the actions of her government in Korea become more and more desperate and cruel.

Korean reactions to this oppression were many and varied. One of the most important was that of the Christians, many of whom refused to obey the order to worship at Japanese Shinto shrines. In 1937, the year this order was promulgated, the minister and many members of a Presbyterian church in P'yongyang were arrested for refusing to obey. In 1939 all Christians who would not worship the Shinto gods were imprisoned, and many of them were tortured. In 1940 a number of Christians were accused of campaigning against the war and put in prison, and in March of 1941, even before the United States entered the war, several dozen British and American missionaries were arrested and secretly interned in a remote area of Kangwon Province.

Many Korean youths attempted to evade conscription, and were sent to the coal mines and munitions factories when caught. Many who were conscripted deserted at the first opportunity. As the situation worsened it became increasingly clear even to many Japanese that the defeat of Japan was inevitable.

The Japanese takeover of Manchuria in 1932 had greatly hampered the activities of patriot groups there. Many of them retreated into China proper, where some joined the forces of the Provisional Government [a government in exile set up by resistance leaders during Japanese rule], while others were won over by the Communists. In 1940 the Provisional Government removed to Chungking, where the Chinese government was then operating, and brought a great many Korean patriot groups under its control. In 1941 it organized a single military force from these, with Yi Pom-sok, a patriot fighter from Manchuria, as commander. At the same time, Korean units were set up within the Chinese Communist forces, which were based at Sian in the northwest. All these forces fought the Japanese side by side with the Chinese, and one Korean unit was even dispatched by the Chinese leader Chiang Kai-shek to aid the British in Burma.

After the Japanese attack on Pearl Harbor brought the United States into the war, the Provisional Government began to make diplomatic contact with the Allied Powers with a view to ensuring Korea's independence after the war. As the Japanese suffered defeat after defeat, hope and joy rose in the hearts of Koreans both at home and abroad.

The day of liberation was surely coming soon.

Driven back from all her Pacific conquests, pounded by perpetual Allied bombing raids and appalled by the tremendous destruction of the atomic bombs dropped on Hiroshima and Nagasaki, the Japanese at last surrendered unconditionally on August 15, 1945. The provisions of the Cairo and Potsdam declarations immediately came into force, and after forty years of struggle against the oppression of rulers who had tried to obliterate her very identity, Korea was free once more. For about three weeks, the Korean people lived in a state of happy confusion, and for many of them it was an emotional experience too deeply felt to be adequately described. Their happiness was soon overshadowed, however, by domestic political differences and the collision of the United States and Soviet Russia.

Tens of thousands of political prisoners came out of the jails as the Japanese relinquished control, and political and social organizations appeared in bewildering variety. The chief differences were between the Nationalists, who were awaiting the return of the Provisional Government leaders, and the Socialists and Communists, who wished to set up a Socialist state. All the differences which had rent the independence movement in the past and even divided the Provisional Government on occasion reappeared in aggravated form once independence became a reality.

Occupation

Meanwhile, arrangements made among the victorious Allies were developing in such a way as to have the gravest consequences for Korea. One of the agreements reached after Russia's entry into the war against Japan had been that, upon a Japanese surrender, Russian troops should occupy Korea north of the thirty-eighth parallel, while those of the United States should occupy the area south of it. On the part of the United States, at any rate, this was thought of as a purely temporary arrangement, until such time as a Korean government could be formed and national elections held under the supervision of the United Nations. It was soon to become clear that the Russians saw it differently.

With the Russian forces already occupying the north, the troops of the United States Eighth Army under the command of Lieutenant General John R. Hodges began to arrive at Inch'on on September eighth. On the following day the Japanese forces officially surrendered in Seoul. The Governor-General was dismissed and the Japanese flag hauled down from the Government-General building. General Archibald V. Arnold was appointed military governor and a military government was organized. The American authorities made it clear from the outset that freedom of political activity was guaranteed and that they would observe strict neutrality in all arrangements made by Koreans in the process of organizing a government and holding elections.

In the north meanwhile, the Russians hastened to set up a Communist government led by Koreans. Cho Man-sik at first headed the Council of People's Commissars, but was soon replaced by Kim Il-song, who then began his long dictatorship. The Korean Provisional Council of People's Commissars was then set up and a Russian-style Communist regime organized. The nature of its rule could easily be judged by the fact that tens of thousands of people fled to the south, accompanied by every Japanese soldier or resident who could escape. Their numbers increased daily, and as the Russians guarded the thirty-eighth parallel more closely their efforts became more desperate.

Members of the Provisional Government now began to arrive in Seoul. Syngman Rhee returned in the middle of October, after a thirty-three-year absence from his homeland. In the latter part of November President Kim Ku and other important leaders arrived. All the nationalist groups supported them, and the people were anxious for the promised elections which were supposed to end the division of the country. They had to declare that they had returned in the capacity of private citizens, however, for the American military government recognized neither the Provisional Government nor the People's Republic which had been set up in the south.

Immediately upon his return, Syngman Rhee said in an interview, "When I heard there were some sixty political parties in Korea while I was preparing to return, my heart ached." He added that the first task for the Korean people was to unify the country and terminate the American and Russian military governments as quickly as possible. As soon as he could, he contacted General Hodges and Military Governor Arnold to urge upon them the importance of a free and united Korea.

The Trusteeship Plan

The division of the country was widely resented, and many of the political parties pressed for an end to it. One of them, the People's Party, even sent a resolution to [U.S.] general [Douglas] MacArthur demanding its abolition. But the Koreans were in for worse trouble. In October came the shocking news that the Allied Powers had decided that Korea was to be ruled by a trusteeship system for a maximum of five years. A provisional government was to be formed under the trusteeship of the United States, Britain, the Soviet Union and China. A conference of the foreign ministers of the United States, Britain and the Soviet Union was to be held in December in Moscow, and two weeks later the American and Russian commanders in Korea should proceed to carry out the arrangement.

Resistance was instantaneous and practically unanimous. After all the years of longing and fighting for independence, the Korean people simply could not accept the idea of even benevolent foreign rule. All the political parties agreed on this point and issued public statements opposing trusteeship. Demonstrations were practically continuous during the last months of 1945, and the press encouraged them in every paper that appeared. The trusteeship arrangements continued, however, and on the last day of the year the streets were still filled with angry people and the shopkeepers had closed their stores in protest.

Then on January 2, 1946, the Communist groups in Korea, doubtless on Russian instruction, suddenly changed their attitude and came out in favor of trusteeship. Well-rehearsed demonstrations in favor of trusteeship were held in north Korea and leftist groups in the south dutifully fell into line, while the nationalists stubbornly maintained their opposition.

In the midst of the continuing political turmoil, preparations went on for a Russo-American conference to organize a provisional government and a House of Representatives was appointed with Syngman Rhee as speaker, to act in a consultative capacity to the U.S. military government. This helped solidify the nationalist groups while the leftists were still trying to organize opposition to them. The trusteeship issue thus had the effect of creating a clear division between left and right.

After several preliminary meetings, the formal conference was held at Toksu palace in March, and almost immediately reached an impasse. The Russian side insisted that no political group or leader that had participated in the anti-trusteeship movement should be allowed to take part in forming the new government, hoping in this way to exclude the nationalists and set up a leftist government which they would be able to control. The American side refused to accept this provision and insisted that, to be truly democratic, the new government should consult all leading groups and shades of opinion. After weeks of fruitless argument, the conference was suspended *sine die* on May eighth.

The American Efforts and the Rise of Syngman Rhee

[U.S.] General Hodges and his staff had not expected to rule a whole nation for any length of time, and despite their goodwill they faced problems with which they were ill prepared to deal. Japanese exploitation and concentration on munitions industries during the war had left the Korean economy a shambles, and in any case most of the nation's heavy industry was in the north and so controlled by the Communists. In addition, some 2,000,000 refugees had poured into the south, mostly from the north but many from China and Japan. Many of what factories there were stood idle because of lack of technical or administrative skills.

The American authorities did what they could, taking control of mines, reforming farm rents, and prohibiting the buying and selling of Japanese property. But they lacked detailed knowledge of civil administration and economics, and their regulations were made on a trial-and-error basis and frequently changed, creating more confusion. The political uproar over trusteeship and the Russo-American Conference was a constant and perplexing problem.

The political situation did clarify somewhat. The Korean People's Party led by Syngman Rhee pushed strongly for national unification and withdrawal of the trusteeship plan. The Korean Independence Party under Kim Ku and other members of the former Provisional Government wanted a national assembly elected and cooperation of all parties against trusteeship. A middle-right group led by Kim Kyu-sik and a middle-left group led by Yo Un-hyong both tried to heal the rift between left and right. But the left, especially the Communists, refused to give up support of trusteeship and demanded that the Russo-American Conference be resumed. When warrants were issued for the arrest of leading Communists on criminal charges, they went underground and began fomenting strikes and riots, the most serious of which were the railway strike in Pusan and the riot of workers in Taegu.

In December of 1946 the Interim Legislature was formed under the American Military Government. Of the forty-five elected members the majority were from the Korean Democratic Party and the People's Council, which was led by Syngman Rhee. An additional forty-five were appointed by the Military Government, mainly from the groups led by Kim Kyu-sik and Yo Un-hyong. It was to propose urgently needed legislation in consultation with the Military Government.

During its first year, the American Military Government used a dual system with joint American and Korean heads of each department. When this proved ineffective, the Americans were changed from heads of departments to advisers. In February 1947, An Chae-hong was appointed Civil Governor, the highest post. In June the military government was officially designated the south Korean Interim Government. A committee on government reorganization was established. A little later So Chae-p'il, who had supported Korean independence fifty years before, returned to offer his services as adviser, and was of great help in establishing a civilian administration. But the Interim Government was subject to many strains and stresses, and there were many problems with which it could not cope. It became daily more obvious that the formation of an independent Korean government was a necessity for the welfare of the people.

United Nations Involvement

The Russo-American Conference meetings were resumed in Seoul in May 1947, at which time the leading political parties presented to it in writing their suggestions for the formation of a provisional government. These suggestions differed so widely and contradicted each other in so many ways that the Conference could find no common ground on which all of them could be included. Moreover, the Russians renewed their insistence that all groups which had opposed the trusteeship plan must be excluded, a position which remained unacceptable to the United States. No real discussions were held, the two sides simply issuing statements from time to time.

Judging that negotiations must be held at a higher level if any progress was to be achieved, the United States proposed calling a foreign ministers' conference of itself, Britain, China and the Soviet Union for the settlement of the Korean problem. When Russia officially refused to accept this proposal, the United States placed the Korean question before the United Nations on September 17, 1947. The United Nations agreed, despite Russian objections, to attempt a solution.

The committee appointed to work on the problem laid before the General Assembly a plan which called, first of all, for general elections throughout Korea under U.N. supervision. When a Korean government had been formed, both Russia and the United States were to withdraw their troops. At the same time, the United Nations Committee for the Unification and Rehabilitation of Korea (UNCURK) was to be organized to advise and consult with the new government. Over continuing Russian objections this plan was accepted by the General Assembly with some slight alterations.

UNCURK began to function in January 1948 and immediately found itself excluded from north Korea by the Russians. In February it was decided to hold elections in the south in accordance with the U.N. resolution. These were held on May 10, when 198 representatives were elected to the National Assembly, 100 seats being left vacant in case of possible future elections in the north. The Assembly held its first session on May 31, and declared that from henceforth the official name of the nation was Taehan Minguk (freely translated as the Republic of Korea) and then set about drawing up a constitution, which was promulgated on July 17. Under this constitution, the Assembly elected Syngman Rhee as the first president of the Republic, and he immediately formed a government. On August 15, 1948, the third anniversary of liberation, the newly formed Republic of Korea was proclaimed to the world. It soon received diplomatic recognition from the United States and about fifty other countries. In December the United Nations proclaimed it the only legitimate government on the Korean peninsula.

The Formation of Communist North Korea

While these events were going forward the last feeble gesture toward peaceful unification ended in failure. Having founded the Korea Council of People's Commissars as a step toward establishing a permanent Communist regime, the north Koreans proposed negotiations between representatives from north and south Korea at P'yongyang in April of 1948. This turned out to be simply a brain-washing operation on the part of the north Koreans, and nothing was achieved. Matters had gone too far for Korea to be unified through negotiations. For the time being, however, there was no overt conflict. The Russo-American Conference was dissolved and by June 1949, both Russian and American troops had been withdrawn.

In defiance of the U.N. resolution the so-called People's Republic of Korea was formed in September 1948. Almost immediately it began harassing guerrilla raids on the south, together with a propaganda campaign and fomenting of riots. Behind the scenes, serious military preparations were pushed forward as fast as possible.

In the south, the new government was having a difficult time. Communist-inspired strikes and riots were frequent, and so much money had to be spent on maintaining public order that shortages of essential goods and inflation followed. A majority of the Assemblymen elected were without political party affiliations, a clear sign of public disenchantment with the politicians. And the Republic's armed forces, which possessed no tanks and no warplanes, were far inferior in strength to the north Korean forces.

The Korean War

It was under these circumstances that early on the morning of June 25, 1950, without any warning or declaration of war, masses of north Korean troops crossed the thirty-eighth parallel and swept down upon the unprepared south. The Republic's troops fought bravely, but proved no match for the heavily armed Communists and the Russian T-34 tanks. The government was forced to move to Pusan and thousands of Seoul citizens fled before the advancing invaders. They were not checked until they reached the Naktong River near Taegu.

The Republic of Korea immediately protested to the United Nations. In response, the Security Council passed a resolution ordering the Communists to withdraw to the thirty-eighth parallel and encouraged all member nations to give military support to the Republic. United States troops soon began to arrive, and were subsequently joined by those of many other nations, including Britain, France, Canada, Australia, the Philippines and Turkey. Under the command of [U.S.] general Douglas MacArthur they began to take the initiative, and after the surprise landing at Inch'on pushed the Communists out of south Korea and advanced into the north. Some units reached the Yalu River, and it seemed unification would at last be realized.

But in October the Communist Chinese intervened. Chinese troops appeared in such large numbers that the U.N. forces were compelled to make a strategic retreat, and Seoul once again fell into Communist hands on January 4, 1951. The U.N. forces regrouped and mounted a counter-attack which re-took Seoul on March 12. A stalemate was reached roughly in the area along the thirty-eighth parallel, where the conflict had begun.

At this point the Russians called for truce negotiations, which finally began at Kaesong in July of 1951 and were transferred to P'anmunjom in November of the same year. These talks were once suspended and dragged on for over a year before agreement was finally reached on July 27, 1953. Against the will of the Republic of Korea, it was agreed that each side should pull its forces back behind a demilitarized zone that was to follow the battle line at the time the armistice went into effect. Prisoners were exchanged and a neutral Supervision Committee was set up to ensure that both sides abided by the agreement. The three years of struggle had resulted in nothing but loss of life and property for both sides, and unification had been rendered virtually impossible without a radical change in the world situation.

The casualties and damage inflicted by the war were heavy. On the U.N. side 150,000 people were killed, 250,000 wounded, 100,000 kidnapped to the north, 200,000 missing and several million homeless. Precise figures are not available for the Communist side, but it is probable that their casualties were far greater. Taken and retaken four times, Seoul lay in ruins, as did most of the other cities of the south. More than half of all industrial facilities were inoperative, countless numbers of roads and bridges were destroyed and whole villages had been wiped out in many areas. But the gravest damage was to the Korean dream of unification. This was no longer a matter only of Korean concern, but had become an issue in the world conflict known as the Cold War. Once again Korea was compelled to suffer from the clash of powers greater than herself.

Kim Il Sung Continues Attacks on South Korea

By Guy R. Arrigoni

Since the division of the Korean peninsula at the end of the Korean War in 1953, North Korea has followed a pattern of infiltration, sabotage, and terror attacks on South Korea as part of a strategy to reunite the two Koreas. As Guy R. Arrigoni describes in this selection, North Korea began by sending military infiltrators into South Korea to obtain intelligence information and foment revolution. In the 1960s North Korea shifted to a more violent strategy, seeking to destabilize South Korea through commando raids and terrorist attacks. In addition to provoking military altercations along the demilitarized zone—the border area between North and South Korea—North Korea has attempted on several occasions to assassinate South Korean presidents and has conducted terrorist attacks against South Korean targets. For example, on October 9, 1983, North Korean agents attempted to assassinate South Korean president Chun Doo Hwan while he was visiting Rangoon, Burma; their bomb, however, exploded prematurely and instead killed eighteen South Korean officials, including four cabinet ministers. Also, on November 29, 1987, North Korea exploded a bomb aboard a Korean Airlines jetliner, killing 115 passengers on board. Arrigoni is a senior analyst for Asian affairs at the U.S. Department of Defense.

Since the division of the peninsula, North Korea has used subversion and sabotage against South Korea as part of its effort at reunification. Historically, the military part of this effort has centered on military infiltration, border incidents designed to raise tensions, and psychological warfare operations aimed at the South Korean armed forces. Infiltration by North Korean military agents was commonplace

---

Guy R. Arrigoni, "National Security," *North Korea: A Country Study*, edited by Andrea Matles Savada. Washington, DC: Library of Congress, 1994.

in South Korea after the armistice in 1953. Over time, however, there were clear shifts in emphasis, method, and apparent goals. P'yongyang [North Korea's capital] initially sent agents to gather intelligence and to build a revolutionary base in South Korea.

North Korea Turns to Violence

The 1960s saw a dramatic shift to violent attempts to destabilize South Korea, including commando raids and incidents along the DMZ [demilitarized zone between the borders of North and South Korea] that occasionally escalated into firefights involving artillery. The raids peaked in 1968, when more than 600 infiltrations were reported, including an unsuccessful commando attack on the South Korean presidential mansion by thirty-one members of North Korea's 124th Army Unit. The unit came within 500 meters of the president's residence before being stopped. During this incident, twenty-eight infiltrators and thirty-seven South Koreans were killed. That same year, 120 commandos infiltrated two east coast provinces in an unsuccessful attempt to organize a Vietnamese-type guerrilla war. In 1969 over 150 infiltrations were attempted, involving almost 400 agents. Thereafter, P'yongyang's infiltration efforts abated somewhat, and the emphasis reverted to intelligence gathering, covert networks, and terrorism.

The Next Step: Terrorism

Subsequent incidents of North Korean terrorism focused on the assassination of the South Korean president or other high officials. In November 1970, an infiltrator was killed while planting a bomb intended to kill South Korean president Park Chung Hee at the Seoul National Cemetery. In 1974 a Korean resident of Japan visiting Seoul killed Park's wife in another unsuccessful presidential assassination attempt.

From the mid-1970s to the early 1980s, most North Korean infiltration was conducted by heavily armed reconnaissance teams. These were increasingly intercepted and neutralized by South Korean security forces.

After shifting to sea infiltration for a brief period in the 1980s, P'yongyang apparently discarded military reconnaissance in favor of inserting agents into third countries. For example, on October 9, 1983, a three-man team from North Korea's intelligence services attempted to assassinate South Korean president Chun Doo Hwan while he was on a state visit to Rangoon, Burma. The remote controlled bomb exploded prematurely. Chun was unharmed, but eighteen South Korean officials, including four cabinet ministers, were killed and fourteen other persons were injured. One of the North Korean agents was killed, two were captured, and one confessed to the incident. On November

29, 1987, a bomb exploded aboard a Korean Air jetliner returning from the Middle East, killing 135 passengers on board. The bomb was placed by two North Korean agents. The male agent committed suicide after being apprehended. The female agent was turned over to South Korean authorities; she confessed to being a North Korean intelligence agent and revealed that the mission was directed by Kim Jong Il as part of a campaign to discredit South Korea before the 1988 Seoul Olympics. In the airliner bombing, North Korea broke from its pattern of chiefly targeting South Korean government officials, particularly the president, and targeted ordinary citizens.

North Korea's Famine and Economic Crisis

By Don Oberdorfer

Beginning in 1995, North Korea began experiencing a series of devastating floods that destroyed agricultural harvests and caused the normally self-sufficient North Korean government to request aid from the United Nations (UN). As described in the following excerpt by Don Oberdorfer, UN workers who visited the country in 1995 found widespread malnutrition and hungry people scavenging for roots and wild plants to feed their families. As Oberdorfer points out, in the past North Korea would have imported food from its Communist allies to cover the food shortage. This time, however, because of the collapse of the Soviet Union and China's own economic problems, such aid was not available. Nor could North Korea borrow money to purchase food from international markets due to its poor credit history.

By 1996 North Korea's economy had virtually collapsed, and by 1998 U.S. officials estimated that perhaps as many as five hundred thousand people had died in North Korea from starvation. Yet throughout the crisis North Korea's leader, Kim Jong Il, emphasized military readiness, causing some observers to fear that instability in North Korea would cause its leaders to become desperate enough to attack South Korea. In the late 1990s, acquiring food aid increasingly became the focus of North Korean diplomacy. The United States and South Korea were thus put in the uncomfortable position of not wanting to prop up a failing North Korean regime yet fearing that a sudden downfall of the regime might bring violence to the region.

Don Oberdorfer is a journalist and scholar at Johns Hopkins University's Nitze School of Advanced International Studies.

Don Oberdorfer, "North Korea in Crisis," *The Two Koreas: A Contemporary History*. New York: Basic Books, 2001. Copyright © 1997 by Don Oberdorfer. Reproduced by permission.

The realization that North Korea was in deep trouble began with an act of nature. On the sticky midsummer day of July 26, 1995, the skies over the country darkened. Rains began to pound the earth, rains that were heavy, steady, and unrelenting and that soon turned into a deluge of biblical proportions. The DPRK [Democratic People's Republic of Korea or North Korea] Bureau of Hydro-Meteorological Service recorded 23 inches of rain in ten days; in some towns and villages, according to the United Nations, as much as 18 inches of rain fell in a single day, bringing floods that were considered the worst in a century.

North Korea Asks for Aid

As a self-proclaimed "socialist paradise," North Korea traditionally had said little or nothing about domestic disasters. This time, as the rains ended in mid-August, it broke its silence and described the tragedy in expansive terms, even exaggerating the admittedly severe impact of the flooding. In late August, for the first time in its history, the bastion of self-reliance openly appealed to the world for help, asking the United Nations [UN] for nearly $500 million in flood relief as well as fuel and medical assistance.

Because the United Nations agencies and other aid-givers had no confidence that aid they sent would reach the country's people, they demanded and obtained access to flood-stricken parts of the North Korean countryside as a condition of providing assistance. This trailblazing access to some previously inaccessible areas was troubling to the secretive DPRK military and security forces, but they had no other choice than to accept it.

Trevor Page, chief of the newly opened UN World Food Program office in Pyongyang, visited the Korean hinterland late in 1995 and found malnutrition rampant and hungry people nearly everywhere. In the western province of Huanghei, Page observed "people scavenging in the fields looking for roots and wild plants to prepare soup for their families. People were anxious, restless. They are not getting enough to eat." Further south near the demilitarized zone [the border zone created between North and South Korea at the end of the Korean War], in one of the country's prime food-producing areas, Page found "not a cabbage to be seen" after authorities reduced the already-minimal food ration under the Public Distribution System to the bare subsistence level: a bowl or two of rice or corn per person per day. Even that was uncertain due to frequent supply failures.

Based on a visit to farming areas, cities, and DPRK government agencies in early December, a team of experts from the UN's Food and Agricultural Organization and its World Food Program reported that the floods "were extremely serious and caused extensive damage to agriculture and infrastructure." The experts also reported, however, that "the floods made an already and rapidly deteriorating food supply situation much worse, rather than caused the situation in the first place."

Underlying Economic and Food Problems

The DPRK had been historically able to till only about one-fifth of its mountainous territory and that usually for only one crop annually, since much of the northern land was frost free only six months of the year. In addition, overuse of chemical fertilizers in desperate pursuit of higher yields, failure to rotate crops, and short-sighted denuding of hillsides that accelerated erosion had all severely affected the country's capacity to grow sufficient food. In the past, Pyongyang had coped with dwindling harvests by importing large amounts of grain under subsidized terms from its communist allies. Such imports were no longer possible when the Soviet Union collapsed and China, whose domestic consumption was rising in a swiftly growing economy, became a grain importer itself and began demanding hard cash for exports to Pyongyang. Despite its need to make up for massive shortfalls of more than 2 million tons of grain in both 1994 and 1995, North Korea lacked the foreign currency or access to credit to do more than very modest buying on international markets.

Long before the floods began, North Korea had been quietly asking selected countries for help in dealing with its food shortage. In the early 1990s, according to the then-director of the ROK [Republic of Korea or South Korea] intelligence agency, Suh Dong Kwon, the North requested 500,000 tons of rice from the South on condition that it be supplied secretly. The idea was dropped after Seoul responded that in its increasingly open society, it would be impossible to hide the rice shipments to the North. After a skimpy harvest in 1992, the regime began to propagandize to the public "Let's Eat Two Meals a Day," a program of austerity. Later, during the 1994 Geneva negotiations with the United States, DPRK officials had spoken with urgency of their severe food problems, but the U.S. team was so fixed on nuclear issues that the comments made little impression. . . .

Economic Collapse

By the winter of 1996, most observers who were following the situation in North Korea had watched the progressive sinking of the economy for many months and had become inured to the adverse trends. Portents of disaster and predictions of impending collapse had become commonplace, yet the North's ability to absorb external and internal reverses had been demonstrated time after time as it accepted the loss of its allies, the death of its founding leader, and the increasingly steep decline in its standard of living. Thus, it seemed possible to assume, in the face of all logic, that the country could continue indefinitely on its downward slope without experiencing a crisis.

Reports from travelers to North Korea, however, suggested this could hardly be the case. In fact, a principal debate among American government analysts was whether the DPRK economy was collapsing or had already collapsed. Deteriorating or flooded coal mines and reduced petroleum imports produced insufficient energy for industry, so many factories had closed or were operating at only a fraction of their previous output. Fuel was so scarce in some provincial cities that only oxcarts and bicycles could be seen on the streets. Many office buildings and dwellings, even in the much-favored capital, were unheated during large portions of a very cold winter. Electrical blackouts were commonplace. Even the state television station was off the air for long periods of time due to lack of power. Many trains, some of them coal-fired and others powered by electricity, were idle. An American intelligence official, who in the past had been sanguine about North Korea's prospects, compared its plight to that of a terminally ill patient, whose physical systems were weakening one after another, with each expiring organ reducing the performance of the others.

A drop in fertilizer production had diminished agricultural yields in the autumn 1996 harvest, adding to the serious shortages caused by flooding. In many cases crops that had been harvested could not be moved to where they were needed due to lack of transport, and more was lost to rain and rats. The meager public distribution of food in the countryside, which averaged three hundred grams per day earlier in the year, was cut back to half or less, barely enough to sustain life, or had stopped completely. To survive, North Koreans were consuming oak leaves, grasses, roots, tree bark, and other nonstandard foods, many with little nutritive value, and buying or bartering food, clothing, and fuel at markets that had sprung up in many towns in violation of government policy. In some areas, dormant factories were being dismantled and turned into scrap metal, which was then bartered across the Chinese border for the cheapest food available.

Kim Jong Il's Response

Although the authorities had no choice but to accept these transgressions and local officials appear to have abetted or even sponsored them, the remarkable thing was that the authority and cohesion of the regime seemed undiminished, so far as the outside world could see.

Song Young Dae, the former ROK vice-minister of national unification and longtime negotiator with the North, described the DPRK scene in late 1996 as "stability within instability," with Kim Jong Il at the top of a crisis-management system controlled by the military. Among the greatest unknown factors was how the trauma of the North Korean economy and society would affect the country's political and military systems.

In these dire circumstances Kim Jong Il paid a visit to Kim Il Sung University on December 7, on the occasion of the fiftieth anniversary of the founding of his alma mater, the nation's foremost institution of higher education. The transcript of his lengthy and rambling remarks, evidently delivered in confidence to several Workers Party secretaries who accompanied him, was brought out of North Korea by Hwang Jang Yop [a high-level North Korean government official who later defected to South Korea], who was not present but who was privy to such materials in his post as a party secretary. The text of the speech was eventually published in *Monthly Chosun* in Seoul. As of the spring of 1997, it was the only record of Kim Jong Il's candid utterances available outside North Korea, except for the tapes surreptitiously made by the kidnapped filmmakers [a husband and wife kidnapped by Kim Jong Il from South Korea to work on North Korea's film industry] over a decade earlier.

In his remarks Kim acknowledged to some extent the difficulties facing the country, saying that "the most urgent issue to be solved at present is the grain problem. . . . the food problem is creating a state of anarchy." Despite the onslaught of "heart-aching occurrences," Kim was highly critical of the street-corner food sellers and peddlers who had spontaneously emerged in response to urgent needs. "This creates egotism among the people, and the base of the party's class may come to collapse. Then, the party will lose popular support and dissolve. This has been well-illustrated by past incidents in Poland and Czechoslovakia."

Kim absolved himself of responsibility for the country's economic problems, maintaining that his father, who had spent much of his time in economic guidance, "repeatedly told me that if I got involved in economic work, I would not be able to handle party and army work properly." He implied that his job was too important to deal with mere economic issues: "If I handle even practical economic work, it will have irreparable consequences on the revolution and construction. . . . The people now unconditionally accept the directives of the Party Central Committee because of my authority, not because party organizations and functionaries carry out their work well. . . . No functionary assists me effectively. I am working alone."

The only institution to win unstinting praise from Kim Jong Il was the army, on which he had become increasingly reliant. Of forty-seven of his activities during 1996 made public in North Korea, thirty were visits to military units or other military-related activities. In contrast to the laggard youth he had observed at Kim Il Sung University, he declared, "all soldiers are politically and ideologically sound and their revolutionary military spirit is lofty." He was satisfied that the soldiers would "protect with their lives the nerve center of the revolution"— himself and other high-level leaders.

Kim's speech confirmed that, as suspected by American and South Korean intelligence, food shortages were affecting even the army. He proclaimed that the people must be told, "If you do not send rice to the army, even if the wretched Americans attack us, we cannot win. Then you will also become slaves, and your sons and daughters and grandsons and granddaughters will too."

North Korea Emphasizes Military Readiness

In January 1997, despite the catastrophic state of the economy, Kim as commander-in-chief ordered a return to the full-scale conduct of the winter training exercises, which had been severely truncated the previous year. At great expense in fuel, ammunition, and other resources, a large proportion of North Korea's huge army moved along the roadways and trails to new positions, fired weapons, and practiced for combat operations. In March, Kim also ordered highly unusual "total mobilization" exercises in which cars in Pyongyang were covered with camouflage netting and thousands of people took refuge in underground shelters, as they would do in case of war. On April 25, the anniversary of the founding of the army, tens of thousands of troops paraded in mass formations in Pyongyang to mark the occasion.

At his headquarters in Seoul, General Tilelli [the U.S. military commander in South Korea] watched the vigorous military activity in the North with deep concern. He was "intuitively" certain, he told me, that the DPRK military forces had been degraded by shortages and the general deterioration affecting the country. On the other hand, U.S. and South Korean forces had been continuously modernized and improved. While this had affected the military balance on the peninsula to the detriment of the North, he said, it was impossible to say by how much. The DPRK military continued to be highly capable, making up in mass what it lacked in modernization, the American commander said, and it "might be the only viable instrument of national power the regime has left."

What worried him and his staff was the possibility that the North

Korean leadership could become so desperate that the combined power of the U.S. and South Korean forces might no longer deter a massive attack. Tilelli was certain that "the explosion," as such an attack was known among his military planners, would fail after a period of bloody and destructive fighting, which would wreak death and destruction in the South but would also destroy much that North Korea had built in its half-century of existence. Given the lack of what Pyongyang's leadership considers other options, said a member of Tilelli's staff, "I don't think a decision to attack would be irrational—though it might turn out to be wrong."

North Korea Negotiates for Aid

Beginning in 1997, the supply of food to alleviate the devastating situation at home became increasingly the central focus of North Korean diplomacy and of international concern, eclipsing other issues. This placed the United States and South Korea, and much of the world at large, in a terrible dilemma. North Korea was continuing to feed and supply a huge and menacing army even while many of its people were hungry or even starving. The regime's statist and short-sighted policies, as much or more than the floods, were to blame for its current crisis, but it refused to undertake major changes in economic policy. Few nations wished to aid such a regime. Yet a growing number of reports placed North Korea on the brink of a great humanitarian disaster, making it intolerable to do nothing to help. Moreover, for strategic reasons and considerations of international stability, most of North Korea's neighbors and the U.S. government as well, wished to stave off the sudden downfall of that regime, fearing it might bring devastating violence that could affect all of Northeast Asia.

The United States was willing to provide funds to purchase food on a humanitarian basis, and proceeded to do so in response to U.N. appeals. However, Washington rejected attempts by North Korean diplomats to link their attendance at peace talks and agreement to various tension-reducing steps to the supply of food assistance. Washington also ruled out supplying the massive amounts of aid that would be required to end the famine. The U.S. problem was essentially political: Congress would not support "aiding" North Korea, but would permit modest contributions to U.N. humanitarian efforts intended to feed its people.

The Response of North Korea's Neighbors

South Korea was less hesitant about linking food to its diplomatic and political objectives. Early in 1997, ROK officials sought to use food as a bargaining chip, supplying or permitting private groups to supply only limited amounts in order to maximize diplomatic leverage over North Korea. As reports of starvation multiplied, however, public pain over the suffering of fellow Koreans brought a shift in government policy. Beginning in the spring, Seoul provided 50,000 tons of food through the Red Cross. In 1998, with a new administration in office, the ROK relaxed most restrictions on the non-governmental supply of food and other aid. In a spectacular consequence of the new policy, Hyundai group founder Chung Ju Yung, who was born in the North, brought 500 head of cattle through the DMZ [demilitarized zone] on June and 501 in October 1998 for starving North Koreans. His private diplomacy led to unprecedented visits by South Korean tourists to the North, and promises of much bigger North-South economic deals to come.

After initial generosity Japan, whose warehouses were bursting with surplus grain, was held back by requests for restraint from Seoul and then by new revelations that several Japanese citizens, including a 13-year-old girl, had been kidnapped by North Korean agents in the 1970s and never returned. North Korea refused to accept responsibility for the kidnappings, and Japan refused to supply more food.

China, which announced modest contributions of grain to North Korea, was believed to be supplying much greater amounts at cut-rate prices and through private barter deals. Customs data suggested that at least 1.2 million tons of grain crossed the China-DPRK border in 1997. China also supplied more than 1 million tons of oil yearly. These flows of Chinese assistance were essential to the survival of the North Korean regime and maintenance of the status quo on the peninsula, which China strongly favored.

The Famine Worsens

A variety of other nations and charitable organizations also contributed food or funds to purchase food. Yet the emergency continued, compounded by a serious drought in the summer of 1997, followed by tidal waves along the western coast that devastated additional growing areas. It was as if nature had conspired with the unyielding economic policies of their government to bedevil the lives of North Koreans.

The scale of the human tragedy was immense, yet impossible to measure with precision in the secretive country. A team of researchers from the Buddhist Sharing Movement interviewed 1,019 refugees from North Korea just across the Chinese border during eight months in 1997–8, and reported that a shocking 27 percent of the family members of the refugees had died since mid-1995. The movement's executive director estimated that 2.5 million people or more may die—"a famine that may be among the worst in human history." U.S. intelligence officials who had been accumulating and examining the evidence told me in September 1998 they had no precise data, but that "certainly hundreds of thousands" of North Koreans had died from starvation or starvation-related illnesses and that 1 million deaths up to that time seemed "not impossible." About the same time, a State Department official with direct responsibility for Korean relations said he believed that "easily more than 500,000 people" had died.

Jasper Becker, a Beijing-based journalist who wrote a book about the 1958–62 Chinese famine that killed at least 30 million people, found a chilling resemblance to that tragedy in the contemporary DPRK. "This is the world's least fashionable humanitarian crisis, but it is probably worse than anything the world has seen for nearly four decades," Becker wrote in 1998. Like the famine in China, Becker attributed the disaster in North Korea principally to government policy.

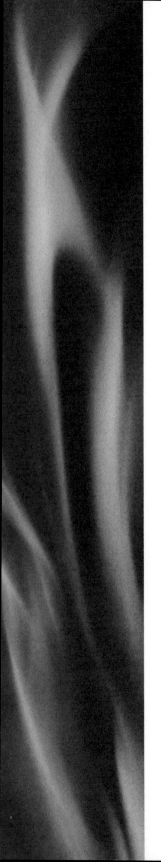

North Korea and Weapons of Mass Destruction

North Korea Is a Terrorist State

By George W. Bush

George W. Bush took office as president of the United States on January 20, 2001. On September 11, 2001, the United States was attacked by terrorists in New York and Washington, D.C., and President Bush responded by announcing a "war on terror" that would be directed not only at terrorists but also at the states that harbor or sponsor them. Thereafter, the United States attacked and destroyed the Taliban regime in Afghanistan that had provided sanctuary to the al-Qaeda terrorists responsible for the September 11 attack.

On January 29, 2002, during his first State of the Union address since the terrorist strike of September 11, 2001, President Bush announced a second phase of the U.S. war on terrorism. In the speech, excerpted below, President Bush states that one of America's goals is to prevent regimes that sponsor terror from threatening the United States or its allies with weapons of mass destruction. Bush specifically identifies three nations—Iraq, Iran, and North Korea—as part of an "axis of evil" that seeks to develop weapons of mass destruction and threaten the peace of the world. The president promises that America will do whatever is necessary to ensure its security. The speech was widely interpreted as the first announcement of a new, preemptive defense policy in which the United States would take action to prevent terrorist groups or countries from developing the means to threaten its security. This was a change from previous U.S. policy, which emphasized only a defensive strategy of using military force after it had been attacked. In early 2003, for the second time since the September 11 attack, President Bush authorized military action against a country that he claimed was a terrorist state. The United States began an attack on the Iraqi regime of Saddam Hussein, which had sought to develop weapons of mass destruction in spite of United Nations prohibitions. Many political observers believe that Bush's "axis of evil"

George W. Bush, State of the Union Address, Washington, DC, January 29, 2002.

speech, and the U.S. actions against Afghanistan and Iraq, caused North Korea to fear that the United States might take military action against it next.

Thank you very much. Mr. Speaker, Vice President Cheney, members of Congress, distinguished guests, fellow citizens: As we gather tonight, our nation is at war, our economy is in recession, and the civilized world faces unprecedented dangers. Yet the state of our Union has never been stronger.

America's War on Terror After September 11

We last met in an hour of shock and suffering. In four short months, our nation has comforted the victims, begun to rebuild New York and the Pentagon, rallied a great coalition, captured, arrested, and rid the world of thousands of terrorists, destroyed Afghanistan's terrorist training camps, saved a people from starvation, and freed a country from brutal oppression.

The American flag flies again over our embassy in Kabul. Terrorists who once occupied Afghanistan now occupy cells at Guantanamo Bay. And terrorist leaders who urged followers to sacrifice their lives are running for their own.

America and Afghanistan are now allies against terror. We'll be partners in rebuilding that country. And this evening we welcome the distinguished interim leader of a liberated Afghanistan: Chairman Hamid Karzai.

The last time we met in this chamber, the mothers and daughters of Afghanistan were captives in their own homes, forbidden from working or going to school. Today women are free, and are part of Afghanistan's new government. And we welcome the new Minister of Women's Affairs, Doctor Sima Samar.

Our progress is a tribute to the spirit of the Afghan people, to the resolve of our coalition, and to the might of the United States military. When I called our troops into action, I did so with complete confidence in their courage and skill. And tonight, thanks to them, we are winning the war on terror. The men and women of our Armed Forces have delivered a message now clear to every enemy of the United States: Even 7,000 miles away, across oceans and continents, on mountaintops and in caves—you will not escape the justice of this nation.

For many Americans, these four months have brought sorrow, and pain that will never completely go away. Every day a retired firefighter returns to Ground Zero, to feel closer to his two sons who died there.

At a memorial in New York, a little boy left his football with a note for his lost father: Dear Daddy, please take this to heaven. I don't want to play football until I can play with you again some day.

Last month, at the grave of her husband, Michael, a CIA officer and Marine who died in Mazur-e-Sharif, Shannon Spann said these words of farewell: "Semper Fi, my love." Shannon is with us tonight.

Shannon, I assure you and all who have lost a loved one that our cause is just, and our country will never forget the debt we owe Michael and all who gave their lives for freedom.

Our cause is just, and it continues. Our discoveries in Afghanistan confirmed our worst fears, and showed us the true scope of the task ahead. We have seen the depth of our enemies' hatred in videos, where they laugh about the loss of innocent life. And the depth of their hatred is equaled by the madness of the destruction they design. We have found diagrams of American nuclear power plants and public water facilities, detailed instructions for making chemical weapons, surveillance maps of American cities, and thorough descriptions of landmarks in America and throughout the world.

What we have found in Afghanistan confirms that, far from ending there, our war against terror is only beginning. Most of the 19 men who hijacked planes on September the 11th were trained in Afghanistan's camps, and so were tens of thousands of others. Thousands of dangerous killers, schooled in the methods of murder, often supported by outlaw regimes, are now spread throughout the world like ticking time bombs, set to go off without warning.

Thanks to the work of our law enforcement officials and coalition partners, hundreds of terrorists have been arrested. Yet, tens of thousands of trained terrorists are still at large. These enemies view the entire world as a battlefield, and we must pursue them wherever they are. So long as training camps operate, so long as nations harbor terrorists, freedom is at risk. And America and our allies must not, and will not, allow it.

Pursuit of Terrorists

Our nation will continue to be steadfast and patient and persistent in the pursuit of two great objectives. First, we will shut down terrorist camps, disrupt terrorist plans, and bring terrorists to justice. And, second, we must prevent the terrorists and regimes who seek chemical, biological or nuclear weapons from threatening the United States and the world.

Our military has put the terror training camps of Afghanistan out of business, yet camps still exist in at least a dozen countries. A terrorist underworld—including groups like Hamas, Hezbollah, Islamic Jihad,

Jaish-i-Mohammed—operates in remote jungles and deserts, and hides in the centers of large cities.

While the most visible military action is in Afghanistan, America is acting elsewhere. We now have troops in the Philippines, helping to train that country's armed forces to go after terrorist cells that have executed an American, and still hold hostages. Our soldiers, working with the Bosnian government, seized terrorists who were plotting to bomb our embassy. Our Navy is patrolling the coast of Africa to block the shipment of weapons and the establishment of terrorist camps in Somalia.

My hope is that all nations will heed our call, and eliminate the terrorist parasites who threaten their countries and our own. Many nations are acting forcefully. Pakistan is now cracking down on terror, and I admire the strong leadership of President Musharraf.

But some governments will be timid in the face of terror. And make no mistake about it: If they do not act, America will.

Regimes That Form an "Axis of Evil"

Our second goal is to prevent regimes that sponsor terror from threatening America or our friends and allies with weapons of mass destruction. Some of these regimes have been pretty quiet since September the 11th. But we know their true nature. North Korea is a regime arming with missiles and weapons of mass destruction, while starving its citizens.

Iran aggressively pursues these weapons and exports terror, while an unelected few repress the Iranian people's hope for freedom.

Iraq continues to flaunt its hostility toward America and to support terror. The Iraqi regime has plotted to develop anthrax, and nerve gas, and nuclear weapons for over a decade. This is a regime that has already used poison gas to murder thousands of its own citizens—leaving the bodies of mothers huddled over their dead children. This is a regime that agreed to international inspections—then kicked out the inspectors. This is a regime that has something to hide from the civilized world.

States like these, and their terrorist allies, constitute an axis of evil, arming to threaten the peace of the world. By seeking weapons of mass destruction, these regimes pose a grave and growing danger. They could provide these arms to terrorists, giving them the means to match their hatred. They could attack our allies or attempt to blackmail the United States. In any of these cases, the price of indifference would be catastrophic.

We will work closely with our coalition to deny terrorists and their state sponsors the materials, technology, and expertise to make and deliver weapons of mass destruction. We will develop and deploy effective missile defenses to protect America and our allies from sudden attack. And all nations should know: America will do what is necessary to ensure our nation's security.

We'll be deliberate, yet time is not on our side. I will not wait on events, while dangers gather. I will not stand by, as peril draws closer and closer. The United States of America will not permit the world's most dangerous regimes to threaten us with the world's most destructive weapons.

Our war on terror is well begun, but it is only begun. This campaign may not be finished on our watch—yet it must be and it will be waged on our watch.

We can't stop short. If we stop now—leaving terror camps intact and terror states unchecked—our sense of security would be false and temporary. History has called America and our allies to action, and it is both our responsibility and our privilege to fight freedom's fight.

North Korea Has Nuclear, Chemical, and Biological Weapons and Missiles to Deliver Them

By John Bolton

In August 2002 the U.S. undersecretary of state for arms control and international security, John Bolton, visited Seoul, South Korea, to emphasize the U.S. intention to defend South Korea against North Korean aggression and promote peace on the Korean peninsula. In his speech, excerpted below, Bolton calls North Korea "a self-created and self-perpetuated tragedy" that is starving its people and strangling its economic development while pursuing military objectives. He calls on North Korea to stop its proliferation of missiles, end its development of weapons of mass destruction, and begin economic and political transformation.

Bolton says America's gravest concern is North Korea's continuing development of weapons of mass destruction (WMD) and its development and export of ballistic missiles. He explains that North Korea has already produced enough plutonium for at least one, and possibly two, nuclear weapons. In addition, North Korea has active chemical and bioweapons programs. Finally, Bolton points out that North Korea is the world's biggest sellers of ballistic missile-related equipment, components, materials, and technical ex-

John Bolton, address before the Korean-American Association, Seoul, South Korea, August 29, 2002.

pertise. Indeed, North Korea's willingness to sell missiles and technology has enabled other dangerous nations, such as Syria, Libya, and Iran, to acquire longer-range missile capabilities.

Distinguished guests, it is a pleasure to speak to you today. I am here representing [U.S.]Secretary Powell to reinforce, indeed celebrate, the rock-solid alliance between the United States and the Republic of Korea. We have stood with you shoulder-to-shoulder in times of peace and war, as you have done with us. We will continue to do so. As President Bush remarked last February 2002 during his visit here: "America will stand firmly with our South Korean allies. We will sustain our obligations with honor. Our forces and our alliance are strong, and this strength is the foundation of peace on the Peninsula." At that time, the President also thanked the people of South Korea for their support in the U.S. war on terrorism in the aftermath of the tragic days of September 11. Almost one year since we were attacked, your continued support in the war on terrorism proves that our alliance is also regional and global. Our cooperation in combating this evil is living testimony to our shared values. . . .

The Republic of Korea has blossomed as a democracy, as a cutting edge high-tech economy, and as an example of impressive social change, not only for Asia but in many ways for the world. This November [2002] the people of this great country will showcase your remarkable democratic transformation by hosting the Community of Democracies meeting. My boss, Secretary Colin Powell, is very much looking forward to participating in this seminal event. There is no better vindication of the Secretary's buoyant optimism about the future of mankind than South Korea's achievements over the last two decades.

In sharp contrast, as the Secretary has said, North Korea is a self-created and self perpetuated tragedy. For decades Pyongyang [the capital of North Korea] has strangled its own economic development and starved its people while building a massive military force armed with missiles and weapons of mass destruction. Without sweeping restructuring to transform itself and its relations with the world, the North's survival is in doubt.

North Korea Must Change

Recently, we have seen hopeful signs of potential change. The revival of North-South dialog and the beginning of discussions with Japan on steps that could lead toward normalization have captured headlines. Perhaps even more importantly DPRK [Democratic People's Republic of Korea, or North Korea] has begun to implement some initial steps at freeing prices and allowing private markets to exist. Whether all this flows from their desperation or their inspiration still is an open question. However, if such reforms continue and expand, the future of the North Korean people could be much brighter.

As Secretary Powell has said, "The past does not have to be the future for Pyongyang and its people. We believe that the light of transformation can start to shine where darkness currently prevails . . . To move this process forward we believe the North should quickly live up to its standing agreements with the South—for example, extending a rail link to the South, establishing free trade zones at Kaesong and elsewhere, as well as reuniting separated family members." President Bush has repeatedly emphasized that we support dialog between the North and the South. He has also made clear that our deepest sympathies lie with the oppressed and starving North Korean people, for whom we have provided the largest amount of humanitarian assistance, this year including 155,000 metric tons of grain.

The North must also begin implementing military confidence building and tension reduction measures. Some 30 kilometers from where I stand lies one of the most dangerous places on Earth—the demilitarized zone. The Joint Parallel [a line of latitude that parallels the equator and marks the division between North and South Korea] serves as a dividing line between freedom and oppression, between right and wrong. The brave forces of our two countries stand ready to defend against an evil regime that is armed to the teeth, including with weapons of mass destruction and ballistic missiles. It is a regime that has just a few miles from Seoul the most massive concentration of tubed artillery and rocketry on earth. We in America must always be cognizant of this enormous conventional threat to the South and especially to the people of your thriving capital.

Change in the North's diplomatic, economic, and security posture is necessary, but not sufficient, for it to join the community of nations. Today, perhaps our gravest concern is Pyongyang's continuing development of weapons of mass destruction and exporting the means to deliver them. I must say personally that this administration has repeatedly put the North on notice that it must get out of the business of proliferation. Nonetheless, we see few, if any, signs of change on this front. Too frequently North Korea acts as if the world will keep looking the other way. Unfortunately, the global consequences of its proliferation activities are impossible to ignore.

Since I am Secretary Powell's senior advisor on Arms Control and International Security, let me provide a panoramic view of North Korea's [weapons of mass destruction] activities—chemical, biological, and nuclear as well as the export of missiles and missile technology—and thus explain to you here in South Korea why we are so concerned and the nature of the challenge I believe we face together.

In regard to chemical weapons, there is little doubt that North Korea has an active program. This adds to the threat to the people of Seoul and to the ROK [Republic of Korea or South Korea]-US frontline troops. Despite our efforts to get North Korea to become a party to the Chemical Weapons Convention, they have refused to do so. Indeed, dating back to 1961, when Kim Il-sung issued a public 'Declaration of Chemicalization'—North Korea has flouted international norms. Both of our governments recognize this threat. In a recent report to Congress, the U.S. government declared that North Korea "is capable of producing and delivering via missile warheads or other munitions a wide variety of chemical agents." A recent Defense White Paper published by the South Korean government concurred, noting that North Korea has a minimum of 2,500 tons of lethal chemicals, and that North Korea is "exerting its utmost efforts to produce chemical weapons."

The news on the biological weapons front is equally disturbing. The governments of both the United States and South Korea are aware that the North possesses an active bioweapons program. Indeed, at times the North has flaunted it. In the 1980s, the North Korean military intensified this effort as instructed by then-President Kim Il-sung, who declared that "poisonous gas and bacteria can be used effectively in war."

Both North and South Korea became signatories to the Biological Weapons Convention in 1987, but only the South has lived up to its commitments under this treaty. Just last month, your country made a historic decision to go further and withdraw from the reservation clause in the Geneva Protocol and wholly prohibit the use of biological weapons.

But what can be said of North Korea? The U.S. government believes that North Korea has one of the most robust offensive bioweapons programs on earth. North Korea to date is in stark violation of the Biological Weapons Convention. The United States believes North Korea has a dedicated, national-level effort to achieve a BW [biological weapons] capability and that it has developed and produced, and may have weaponized, BW agents in violation of the Convention. North Korea likely has the capability to produce sufficient quantities of biological agents within weeks of a decision to do so.

Let's turn our attention now to the nuclear question. The U.S. has had serious concerns about North Korea's nuclear weapons program for many years. In a recent report to Congress, the U.S. Intelligence

Community stated that "North Korea has produced enough plutonium for at least one, and possibly two nuclear weapons." Moreover, "Pyongyang continued its attempts to procure technology worldwide that could have application in its nuclear program."

It is true that North Korea has frozen plutonium production activities at the Yongbyon facility as required by the Agreed Framework of 1994 and has allowed a large number of spent fuel rods that could otherwise be used to make nuclear weapons to be stored safely under international supervision. Still these important steps are only part of the agreement. Outstanding concerns remain. To signal our concerns about these unresolved questions, President Bush, for the first time since the signing of the Agreement in 1994, this year did not certify to the U.S. Congress that North Korea is in compliance with all provisions.

"What Is North Korea Hiding?"

The fact is that North Korea has not begun to allow inspectors with the International Atomic Energy Agency to complete all of their required tasks. Many doubt that North Korea ever intends to fully comply with its NPT [Nuclear Non-Proliferation Treaty] obligations. Whatever one thinks, the bottom line is that North has delayed for years bringing the required safeguards agreement into force.

Pyongyang's record of the past 8 years does not inspire confidence. It has gone so far as to demand compensation for lost power generation, when its self-constructed barriers are largely to blame for construction delays. If the North has nothing to hide, then full cooperation with the [International Atomic Energy Agency], as required by its Safeguards Agreement and under the Agreed Framework, should be an easy task. Opening up to IAEA inspectors is the best way to remove suspicions and ensure the delivery of the light water reactors in a timely fashion.

The math is simple. Earlier this month, concrete was poured at Kumho, the facility where the light water reactors are to be built. Construction of a significant portion of the first LWR [light water reactor] is now scheduled to be complete by May 2005, at which time the construction schedule calls for delivery of controlled nuclear components. The problem is that key nuclear components to power the reactors cannot and will not be delivered until the IAEA effectively accounts for North Korea's nuclear activities—past and perhaps present. The IAEA estimates that these inspections will take at least three to four years with full cooperation from North Korea. It is now late summer 2002. Every day that the North fails to allow unfettered IAEA inspections necessarily pushes back the possible completion of the light water reactors.

Continued intransigence on the part of Pyongyang only begs the question: What is North Korea hiding? The concerns of the international community are only deepened by the clear discrepancy between the amount of plutonium that may have been reprocessed at the Yongbyon facility and the amount Pyongyang declared to the IAEA in 1992. The IAEA declared the North's explanations inadequate. As you recall, when the IAEA wanted to inspect waste sites in North Korea in 1992 to help construct the history of the North's nuclear program, the sites were deemed off-limits. If the North's IAEA declarations were accurate, then why not allow verification to occur?

The North could easily answer this question if it complied with the IAEA inspections required under the NPT. In a notable step backward just this past June [2002], however, North Korea withdrew its agreement to discuss the Verification of Completeness and Correctness of the initial declaration of plutonium with the IAEA. This must be changed. If the North is serious and not just using delaying tactics, then it must let the IAEA do its job.

North Korea needs to fulfill its pledge to Seoul when it committed itself to a nuclear free peninsula by signing the Joint North-South Denuclearization Agreement of 1992. That accord mandated random reciprocal inspections and committed both North and South to a nuclear-free peninsula. The South has lived up to its end of the bargain and the North has been handed a real opportunity to improve the welfare of its people and stability on the Peninsula. If the North is serious about peace and reconciliation, then it will do the same.

North Korea's Global Missile Threat

In addition to its disturbing WMD activities, North Korea also is the world's foremost peddler of ballistic missile-related equipment, components, materials, and technical expertise. As the CIA publicly reports: "North Korea has assumed the role as the missile and manufacturing technology source for many programs. North Korean willingness to sell complete systems and components has enabled other states to acquire longer range capabilities." It has an impressive list of customers spanning the globe from the Middle East, South Asia to North Africa, with notable rogue-state clients such as Syria, Libya and Iran.

President Bush's use of the term "Axis of evil" to describe Iran, Iraq, and North Korea was more than a rhetorical flourish—it was factually correct. First, the characteristics of the three countries' leadership are much the same: the leaders feel only they are important, not the people. Indeed, in North Korea, the people can starve as long as the leadership is well fed. Second, there is a hard connection between these regimes—an "axis"—along which flow dangerous weapons and dangerous technology.

Let us use the case of Iran. For some years now, North Korea has provided Iran—arguably the most egregious state sponsor of terror—with medium-range ballistic missiles known as No Dongs. Iran has used this assistance and technology to strengthen its Shahab-3 program. The proliferation relationship may work in reverse, and the fruits of this cooperation could be offered for sale on the international market. Exports of ballistic missiles and related technology are one of the North's major sources of hard currency, which fuel continued missile development and production.

North Korea Must Choose Its Future

North Korea today faces a choice. If North Korea wants to have a brighter future, it needs to fundamentally shift the way it operates at home and abroad. After all, the Soviet Union had 30,000 nuclear warheads and in the end it still collapsed due to its own contradictions.

Working in lockstep with our allies, South Korea and Japan, the United States is prepared to take big steps to help the North transform itself and move our relations toward normalcy. However, our actions in large part will be incumbent on the DPRK's positive movement across a number of fronts. Among other steps, we insist that the North get out of the missile proliferation business. As President Bush has said, "We cannot permit the world's most dangerous regimes to export the world's most dangerous weapons." Also, the North must open up to IAEA inspection and show that it is committed to a nuclear free peninsula. This is what the Agreed Framework was intended to achieve. If the DPRK fails to do so promptly, the future of the Agreed Framework will be in serious doubt.

Last but certainly not least, simple decency demands that the North alleviate the suffering and malnutrition of its citizens. To help the people of North Korea, the US remains committed to the World Food Program's operations in the DPRK. With much better monitoring and access, we could do even more. But international charity alone can't save the North Korean people from tragedy. Economic and political transformation are vital.

During his visit in February [2002] to South Korea, President Bush made our intentions clear. He stipulated that we have no intention of invading North Korea. Rather, he said, "We're prepared to talk with the North about steps that would lead to a better future, a future that is more hopeful and less threatening." We continue to stand by this offer of dialogue—anytime, anyplace.

Today, however, as President Bush stressed, the stability of the Peninsula is built on the successful and strong alliance between the ROK-US. No matter what the future holds, we will stand by the government and people of South Korea.

North Korea's New Nuclear Weapons Threats: Crisis and Opportunity

By James T. Laney and Jason T. Shaplen

In October 2002 North Korea admitted to the United States that it had begun building a new, highly enriched uranium (HEU) nuclear program. In December 2002 North Korea announced it would restart its plutonium-based nuclear program, which was frozen under a 1994 agreement in which it agreed not to develop nuclear weapons. In the following article James T. Laney and Jason T. Shaplen claim that North Korea's October and December 2002 announcements could lead to a dangerous crisis. Alternately, these admissions could also create an opportunity for the United States to negotiate a better deal with North Korea than the 1994 agreement.

Laney and Shaplen note that, prior to the October admission, North Korea had undertaken a number of positive initiatives and may have decided to reveal its nuclear program as a way of keeping the United States engaged in negotiations. Whatever the motivation, North Korea's admission could be viewed as a blessing in disguise that allows the United States to scrap the 1994 Framework Agreement. In its place, the authors argue, the four big powers (United States, Japan, China, and Russia) plus South Korea should negotiate a new deal with North Korea in which they guarantee North Korea's security in exchange for a comprehensive agreement in which North Korea would agree to give up its nuclear weapons programs, end its missile program, reduce its conventional troops along the demilitarized zone between North and South Korea, and implement economic and market reforms. Such

---

James T. Laney and Jason T. Shaplen, "How to Deal with North Korea," *Foreign Affairs*, March/April 2003. Copyright © 2003 by the Council on Foreign Relations, Inc. Reproduced by permission of the publisher.

a deal, Laney and Shaplen argue, provides North Korea with security while addressing the concerns of the other parties. If North Korea balks at this offer, the authors maintain, then the United States is in a better position to pursue tougher options.

Laney served as U.S. ambassador to South Korea from 1993 to 1997, is president emeritus of Emory University, and is cochairman of an independent task force on managing change on the Korean peninsula sponsored by the Council on Foreign Relations. Shaplen was policy adviser at the Korean Peninsula Energy Development Organization from 1995 to 1999 and is also a member of the Council on Foreign Relations task force.

Progress in reducing tensions on the Korean peninsula, never easy, has reached a dangerous impasse. The last six months have witnessed an extraordinary series of events in the region that have profound implications for security and stability throughout Northeast Asia, a region that is home to 100,000 U.S. troops and three of the world's 12 largest economies.

The New North Korea Nuclear Crisis

Perhaps the most dramatic of these events was North Korea's December [2002] decision to restart its frozen plutonium-based nuclear program at Yongbyon [a city in North Korea]—including a reprocessing facility that separates plutonium for nuclear weapons from spent reactor fuel. Just as disturbing was the North's stunning public admission two months earlier [October 2002] that it had begun building a new, highly-enriched-uranium (HEU) nuclear program. And then came yet another unsettling development: a growing, sharp division emerged between the United States and the new South Korean government over how to respond.

But recent events have not been entirely negative. In the two months prior to the October HEU revelation, North Korea had, with remarkable speed, undertaken an important series of positive initiatives that seemed the polar opposite of its posturing on the nuclear issue. These included initiating an unscheduled meeting between its foreign minister, Paek Nam Sun, and Secretary of State Colin Powell in July [2002]—the highest-level contact between the two nations since the Bush administration took office; inviting a U.S. delegation for talks in Pyongyang; proposing the highest-level talks with South Korea in a year; agreeing to re-establish road and rail links with the South and starting work on the project almost immediately; demining portions of the demilitarized zone (DMZ) and wide corridors on the east and west coasts surrounding the rail links; sending more than 600 athletes and representatives to join the Asian Games in Pusan, South Korea (marking the North's first-ever participation in an international sporting event in the South); enacting a series of economic and market reforms (including increasing wages, allowing the price of staples to float freely, and inaugurating a special economic zone similar to those in China); restarting the highest-level talks with Japan in two years; holding a subsequent summit with Japanese Prime Minister Junichiro Koizumi, during which Pyongyang admitted abducting Japanese citizens in the 1970s and 1980s; and finally, allowing the surviving abductees to visit Japan.

Viewed individually, let alone together, North Korea's initiatives represented the most promising signs of change on the peninsula in decades. Whether by desire or by necessity, the North finally appeared to be responding to the long-standing concerns of the United States, South Korea, and Japan. Equally important, Pyongyang seemed to have abandoned its policy of playing Washington, Seoul, and Tokyo off one another by addressing the concerns of one while ignoring those of the other two. For the first time, the North was actively (even aggressively) engaging all three capitals simultaneously.

Until October, that is, when North Korea acknowledged the existence of its clandestine HEU program—ending the diplomatic progress instantly. Once the news broke, Pyongyang quickly offered to halt the HEU program in exchange for a nonaggression pact with the United States. But Washington, unwilling to reward bad behavior, initially refused to open a dialogue unless the North first abandoned its HEU effort. In November, the United States went a step further: saying that Pyongyang had violated the 1994 Agreed Framework and several other nuclear nonproliferation pacts, Washington engineered the suspension of deliveries of the 500,000 tons of heavy fuel oil sent to the North each year under the 1994 accord. The Agreed Framework had frozen the North's plutonium program—a program that had included a five-megawatt experimental reactor, two larger reactors under construction, and the reprocessing facility—narrowly averting a catastrophic war on the Korean Peninsula.

Further Escalation of the Crisis

In the weeks following the suspension of fuel shipments, the United States hardened its stance against dialogue with the North—despite the fact that most U.S. allies were encouraging a diplomatic solution to the situation. North Korea responded by announcing plans to reopen its Yongbyon facilities. It immediately removed the seals and monitoring cameras from its frozen nuclear labs and reactors and, a few days later, began to move its dangerous spent fuel rods out of storage.

Pyongyang subsequently announced its intention to reopen the critical reprocessing plant in February 2003. On December 31, it expelled the inspectors of the International Atomic Energy Agency (IAEA). And on January 9, it announced its withdrawal from the nuclear Nonproliferation Treaty.

Although Washington, strongly urged by Seoul and Tokyo, ultimately agreed to talks, the situation appeared to be worsening almost daily. Depending on how it is resolved, the standoff could still prove a positive turning point in resolving one of the world's most dangerous flash points. But it could also lead to an even worse crisis than in 1994. The proper approach, therefore, is to now re-engage with North Korea without rewarding it for bad behavior. Working together, the major external interested parties (China, Japan, Russia, and the United States) should jointly and officially guarantee the security of the entire Korean Peninsula. But the outside powers should also insist that Pyongyang abandon its nuclear weapons program before offering it any enticements. Only when security has been established (and verified by intrusive, regular inspections) should a prearranged comprehensive deal be implemented—one that involves extensive reforms in the North, an increase in aid and investment, and, eventually, a Korean federation.

North Korea's Reasons for Going Nuclear

To understand how the most promising signs of progress in decades quickly deteriorated into nuclear brinkmanship, it is necessary to first understand the origins and motivation behind the North's HEU program and Pyongyang's subsequent decision to restart its plutonium program. Even before North Korea admitted that it was building a new HEU program, the United States had long suspected the country of violating its relevant international commitments. Three years ago [1998], such concerns had led to U.S. inspections of suspicious underground facilities in Kumchang-ni. Although those inspections did not reveal any actual treaty violations—in part because Pyongyang had ample time to remove evidence before the inspectors arrived—suspicions lingered. These doubts proved justified in July 2002, when the United States conclusively confirmed the existence of the North's HEU program.

It now seems likely that Pyongyang actually started its HEU program in 1997 or 1998. Although Kim Jong Il's motives for doing so will probably never be clear (his regime has a record of confounding observers), there are two plausible explanations. The first focuses on fear: namely, North Korea's fear that, having frozen its plutonium-based nuclear program in 1994, it would receive nothing in return. Such a suspicion seems unreasonable on its face, since, under the 1994 Agreed Framework negotiated with Washington, Pyongyang was to be compensated in various ways for abandoning its nuclear ambitions. But from the perspective of a paranoid, isolated regime such as North Korea's, this concern was not without justification. Almost from its inception, the provisions of the 1994 accord fell substantially behind schedule—most notably in the construction of proliferation-resistant light-water reactors in the North and improved relations with the United States. North Korea may thus have started its HEU program as a hedge against the possibility that it had been duped, or, more likely, that new U.S., South Korean, or Japanese administrations would be less willing to proceed with the politically controversial program than were their predecessors.

A second, darker, and more likely explanation for Pyongyang's decision to start the HEU program holds that the North never really intended to give up its nuclear ambitions. Whether motivated by fear,

honor, or aggression (the determination to stage a preemptive strike if threatened), Pyongyang views a nuclear program as its sovereign right—and a necessity.

Whichever of these theories is true, the North seems to have undertaken its HEU program slowly at first, ramping it up only in late 2000 or 2001. And it was able to hide the program until July 2002, when U.S. intelligence proved its existence. Although Bush administration officials insist otherwise, it is possible, as North Korean officials have suggested, that Pyongyang decided to step up its nuclear program in response to what it perceived as Washington's increasingly hostile attitude—a hostility demonstrated to North Koreans by President Bush's decision to include them in the "axis of evil" and to set the bar for talks impossibly high. This perceived hostility was further encouraged when the administration announced its new doctrine of preemptive defense. Notwithstanding the president's remarks to the contrary, Pyongyang views the new defense doctrine as a direct threat. After all, if Washington is willing to attack Iraq, another isolated nation with a suspected nuclear program, might it not also be willing, even likely, to do the same to North Korea?

This fear helps explain why the North decided to restart its plutonium program. Many within the senior ranks of the North Korean military believe that if the United States attacks, Pyongyang's position will be strengthened immeasurably by the possession of several nuclear weapons. North Korean planners thus reason that they should develop such weapons as quickly as possible, prior to the American attack that may come once Washington has concluded its war with Iraq.

North Korea's Reasons for Revealing Its Nuclear Program

There are again two plausible explanations for why the North revealed its HEU program in October 2002. Since its earliest days in office, the Bush administration has made clear that it favors a more hard-line approach to North Korea than did the Clinton team. Even prior to the North's HEU admission, Bush's support for the 1994 Agreed Framework was lukewarm at best. His administration considered the accord a form of blackmail signed by his predecessor—even though, after a long review of North Korea policy in 2001, the Bush administration found it could not justify abandoning the pact without having something better with which to replace it. In short, Washington grudgingly considered itself bound by a diplomatic process it viewed as distasteful—if not an outright scam.

When U.S. Assistant Secretary of State James Kelly visited North

Korea in early October, he took with him undeniable evidence of the North's HEU program. He also took with him very narrowly defined briefing papers, hard-line marching orders that reflected the influence of the Defense Department and the National Security Council.

Anticipating isolation and a worsening of already strained relations in the face of Washington's evidence, Pyongyang opted to play one of its few remaining trump cards: open admission of its nuclear program. This openness, Kim may have hoped, would keep the Bush administration from disengaging entirely. By acknowledging its HEU effort, Pyongyang essentially sent Washington the following message: "We understand that despite everything we've done over the past several months you want to isolate or disengage from us. Well, we admit we have a uranium-based nuclear program. You say you don't want to deal with us. Too bad—you can't ignore a potential nuclear power. Deal with us."

Another hypothesis to explain the timing is that Pyongyang simply miscalculated. North Korea watchers learned long ago to expect the unexpected, but even the most jaded observers were surprised in September 2002 when Kim admitted to Koizumi that the North had abducted 13 Japanese in the 1970s and 1980s to train its spies. Kim apologized for the abductions and, with remarkable speed, subsequently authorized a visit of five of the surviving abductees to Japan. In doing so, he removed a decades-old barrier to normalization of relations between the two nations (and to the payment of billions of dollars in hoped-for war reparations from Tokyo).

Kim's gamble on coming clean about the abductions appeared at the time to have paid off. Notwithstanding the predicted public backlash in Japan, further talks between Tokyo and Pyongyang took place in October (after the HEU admission). Having experienced better-than-expected results in admitting to the abductions, Kim may have hoped for the same by confessing to his HEU program. His thinking may have been that, in view of Washington's evidence, Pyongyang would eventually have had to come clean anyway. That being the case, it was better to do so sooner rather than later, thereby removing one of the primary obstacles to improved U.S.–North Korea relations. Kim may further have surmised that the timing of such a revelation in October was advantageous, given recent progress in talks with Japan and South Korea. He probably hoped that Tokyo and Seoul would pressure Washington to mitigate its response.

Policy Options

In the weeks immediately following Kelly's visit, Washington made it clear that it did not see a military solution to the crisis on the Korean Peninsula. This left isolation, containment, and negotiation as the only viable alternatives. A policy of isolation would seek the North's collapse but would not address the HEU problem and would likely result in the North's restarting its plutonium-based nuclear program. Containment, or economic pressure designed to squeeze the North, would seek to punish Pyongyang while leaving the door open to future negotiation. It too would not address the HEU problem but, it was hoped, might maintain the freeze on the plutonium program. Negotiations, meanwhile, would seek to address the nuclear problem but could be viewed by some as a reward for bad behavior.

If a successful isolation or containment policy wins the day, the North will have miscalculated in coming clean. If, however, a policy of dialogue and subsequent negotiation ultimately emerges—or if isolation or containment fails (in part because Washington is unable to persuade China, South Korea, and Russia to endorse it over a sustained period)—Kim will have played his cards exceedingly well.

The Urgency of the Threat

The timing of the steps now taken to resolve the current crisis will be crucial to their success. Indeed, timing is important to understand because the North's HEU program does not pose an immediate threat. Although it has the potential to eventually produce enough uranium for one nuclear weapon per year, it has not yet reached this stage and is not expected to do so for at least two to three more years, according to administration officials and the Central Intelligence Agency.

The North's decision to reopen its plutonium-based nuclear program at Yongbyon poses a more critical and immediate threat, however. Prior to its suspension in 1994, most experts believe this program had already produced enough plutonium for one or two nuclear weapons. The 8,000 spent fuel rods from the five-megawatt reactor contained enough plutonium for an additional four to five nuclear weapons. The IAEA monitored the freeze via seals, cameras, and on-site inspectors. It also canned the 8,000 existing spent fuel rods, placed them in a safe-storage cooling pond, and monitored them until its inspectors were expelled from North Korea on December 31.

The five-megawatt reactor, when operational, will produce enough plutonium for one or two additional nuclear weapons per year. But the 8,000 rods represent an even more immediate challenge. If the North follows through on its threat to reopen the reprocessing facility in February, it would take just six months to reprocess all of its spent fuel and extract enough plutonium to make four or five additional weapons. This would bring Pyongyang's nuclear arsenal to between five and seven weapons by the end of July. It could have enough plutonium for one to three weapons even sooner.

Thus there exists only a short window of opportunity before the North's recent action translates into additional nuclear-weapons material on the ground. The trick to unraveling the current impasse is to avoid rewarding the North for its violations of past treaties with a new, more comprehensive agreement. Blackmail cannot and should not be condoned. The starting point for future discussions should therefore be that the North must completely and immediately abandon its HEU and plutonium-based programs. This pledge must be accompanied by intrusive, immediate, and continuous inspections by the IAEA.

"Blessing in Disguise"

It is a tenet of all international negotiations, however—particularly those that involve the Korean Peninsula—that all crises create opportunity, and this one is no different. At its core—politics stripped aside—the current standoff will allow Washington to scrap the flawed Agreed Framework and replace it with a new mechanism that better addresses the concerns of the United States and its allies. In many ways, the North's HEU admission and its subsequent decision to reopen its plutonium program might therefore be viewed as a blessing in disguise. The Bush administration can finally rid itself of a deal it never liked and never truly endorsed and replace it with one that addresses all of Washington's central concerns, including the North's missile program and its conventional forces. Washington must, however, be willing to make such a deal attractive to the North as well.

Yet timing poses an immediate barrier to negotiating a new mechanism. Pyongyang has insisted it will give up its HEU and plutonium programs only after Washington signs a nonaggression pact with it. But the Bush administration, while publicly reassuring the North that it has no intention of invading, has justifiably insisted that Pyongyang give up these programs before there is any discussion of a new mechanism. The North seems unwilling to lose face by giving up this trump card without a security guarantee, and Washington is unwilling to take any action that appears to reward Pyongyang before it has fully dismantled its nuclear programs.

Those who think they can outwait Pyongyang by isolating it or pressuring it economically, as the Bush administration proposed in late December, are likely to be proved wrong. North Koreans are a fiercely proud people and have endured hardships over the last decade that would have led most other countries to implode. It would therefore be a mistake to underestimate their loyalty to the state or to Kim Jong Il. When insulted, provoked, or threatened, North Koreans will not hesitate to engage in their equivalent of a holy war. Their ideology is not only political, it is quasi-religious. Pyongyang also enjoys an inherent advantage in any waiting game: Beijing. Although China might initially support a policy of economic pressure, Beijing is afraid that it will face a massive influx of unwanted refugees across the Yalu River should the North collapse. To guard against this event, it will ultimately allow fuel and food (sanctioned or unsanctioned) to move across its border with the North. Similarly, South Korea, which also wants to avoid a massive influx of refugees, is unlikely to support a sustained, indefinite policy of squeezing the North. In mid-December, it elected by a larger margin than predicted a new president who ran specifically on a platform of expanding engagement with Pyongyang.

The Best Solution

The way to cut the Gordian knot of who goes first is through a two-stage approach. The first stage would provide the North with the security it craves while also ensuring that Pyongyang is not rewarded for its bad behavior. To achieve this end, the four outside interested powers (the United States, Japan, China, and Russia—each of which has supported one side or the other in the past) would jointly and officially guarantee the security and stability of the entire Korean Peninsula. Washington may not be able or willing to convene a meeting of the four powers to this end. If not, back channels or unofficial initiatives should be used to encourage Moscow or Beijing to take the lead. Both Russia and China have sought to increase their influence on the Korean Peninsula in recent years. This plan would solidify their places at the table.

Once the security of the peninsula has been guaranteed by the outside powers, it will be time for stage two: a comprehensive accord, again broken into two parts. The North must completely give up its HEU and plutonium programs and allow immediate, intrusive, and continuous inspections by the IAEA; end its development, production, and testing of long-range missiles in exchange for some financial compensation; draw down its conventional troops along the DMZ (although there will be no reduction of U.S. troops at this time, and only a very limited reduction of U.S. troops in five years, should the situation permit); and, finally, continue to implement economic and market reforms.

In exchange for the above, Japan would normalize its relations with the North within 18 months of the agreement's coming into effect. This normalization would include the payment of war reparations in the form of aid, delivered on a timetable extending five to seven years. Both halves of the peninsula would also enter a Korean federation within two years of the agreement's coming into effect. And as soon as the IAEA had verified that the North has dismantled its nuclear weapons programs, Washington would sign a nonaggression pact with

Pyongyang. This pact, which by prior agreement would automatically be nullified by subsequent signs that the North was not cooperating or was initiating a new nuclear program, would include the gradual lifting of economic sanctions over three years.

The United States, South Korea, Japan, and the European Union—the primary members of the Korean Peninsula Energy Development Organization (or KEDO, which was set up to administer the Agreed Framework)—would further maintain the organization and provide the two new light-water reactors stipulated in the original deal. KEDO would also resume delivery of heavy fuel oil until the first reactor was completed.

In addition to the above measures, China and Russia would agree to support the North economically via investment. All outside parties to the deal—the United States, South Korea, Japan, China, and Russia—would also contribute to the compensation the North would receive in return for ending its long-range missile program.

Finally, five years after the above accord is signed, a Northeast Asia Security Forum, consisting of the four major powers plus South and North Korea, would be created to ensure long-term peace and stability throughout the region. . . .

[This process] will address the major concerns of all the parties involved. It will assure North Korea of the underlying security it seeks, without requiring Washington to sign a nonaggression pact until after Pyongyang has dismantled its HEU and plutonium programs. If the North balks despite a security guarantee by all major outside powers and the prospect of a comprehensive accord, isolation or economic pressure by Washington and its allies will not only remain a viable alternative, it will be stronger and more fully justified than it would be otherwise, and will more easily win the unified, sustained support of major players in the region. The upside to exploring the path presented above is therefore massive, and the downside very limited. Doing nothing, meanwhile, could become the most dangerous option of all.

U.S. Policy Toward North Korea Is Vicious and Hostile

By the Democratic People's Republic of Korea

Following North Korea's October 2002 announcement that it had a nuclear weapons program, North Korea sought bilateral negotiations and a nonaggression treaty with the United States as a solution to the crisis. The United States rejected this demand and instead cut off fuel and oil supplies to North Korea, threatened sanctions and other punitive actions, and sought multinational negotiations with North Korea that would include South Korea and China. In response, North Korea further escalated international tensions by various provocative actions, including expelling international inspectors from the country and starting up a nuclear reactor that had been shut down as part of the U.S.–North Korea 1994 Framework Agreement on nuclear arms.

In addition, in January 2003 North Korea (whose formal name is the Democratic People's Republic of Korea) announced that it was withdrawing from the Nuclear Non-Proliferation Treaty (NPT), the main means by which the United States and other countries seek to control nuclear weapons proliferation. In its official announcement of this action, reprinted below, North Korea claims that U.S. policy is vicious and hostile and that the United States is seriously violating its state security. Specifically, North Korea denounces a resolution of the International Atomic Energy Association (IAEA) that calls on North Korea to end its nuclear program and allow inspections of its facilities. In addition, North Korea criticizes the United States for listing it as part of an "axis of evil," targeting it for "pre-emptive nuclear attack," violating the 1994 Framework Agreement, and stopping the supply of heavy oil to North Korea. North Korea also claims that the United States has responded to its sincere proposal for negotiations with threats of a "blockade" and "military punishment." If the United States drops its hostile policy toward North

Democratic People's Republic of Korea, statement on NPT withdrawal, January 10, 2003.

Korea, the announcement states, North Korea will show that it is not making nuclear weapons.

A dangerous situation where our nation's sovereignty and our state's security are being seriously violated is prevailing on the Korean Peninsula due to the US vicious hostile policy towards the DPRK [Democratic People's Republic of Korea, or North Korea].

The United States Manipulates the IAEA

The United States instigated the International Atomic Energy Agency (IAEA) to adopt another "resolution" against the DPRK on 6 January [2003] in the wake of a similar "resolution" made on 29 November, 2002.

Under its manipulation, the IAEA in those "resolutions" termed the DPRK "a criminal" and demanded it scrap what the US called a "nuclear programme" at once by a verifiable way in disregard of the nature of the nuclear issue, a product of the US hostile policy towards the DPRK, and its unique status in which it declared suspension of the effectuation of its withdrawal from the Nuclear Non-Proliferation Treaty (NPT).

Following the adoption of the latest "resolution", the IAEA director general issued an ultimatum that the agency would bring the matter to the UN Security Council to apply sanctions against the DPRK unless it implements the "resolution" in a few weeks.

This clearly proves that the IAEA still remains a servant and a spokesman for the US and the NPT is being used as a tool for implementing the US hostile policy towards the DPRK aimed to disarm it and destroy its system by force.

A particular mention should be made of the fact that the IAEA in the recent "resolution" kept mum about the US which has grossly violated the NPT and the DPRK-US agreed framework, but urged the DPRK, the victim, to unconditionally accept the US demand for disarmament and forfeit its right to self-defence, and the agency was praised by the US for "saying all what the US wanted to do." This glaringly reveals the falsehood and hypocrisy of the signboard of impartiality the IAEA put up.

The DPRK government vehemently rejects and denounces this "resolution" of the IAEA, considering it as a grave encroachment upon our country's sovereignty and the dignity of the nation.

It is none other than the US which wrecks peace and security on the

Korean Peninsula and drives the situation there to an extremely dangerous phase.

After the appearance of the Bush administration, the United States listed the DPRK as part of an "axis of evil", adopting it as a national policy to oppose its system, and singled it out as a target of preemptive nuclear attack, openly declaring a nuclear war.

Systematically violating the DPRK-US Agreed Framework, the US brought up another "nuclear suspicion" and stopped the supply of heavy oil, reducing the [Agreed Framework, a 1994 agreement in which North Korea agreed to freeze nuclear weapons development in exchange for oil and light water reactors] to a dead document. It also answered the DPRK's sincere proposal for the conclusion of the DPRK-US non-aggression treaty and its patient efforts for negotiations with such threats as "blockade" and "military punishment" and with such an arrogant attitude as blustering that it may talk but negotiations are impossible.

The US went so far to instigate the IAEA to internationalize its moves to stifle the DPRK, putting its declaration of a war into practice. This has eliminated the last possibility of solving the nuclear issue of the Korean Peninsula in a peaceful and fair way.

It was due to such nuclear war moves of the US against the DPRK and the partiality of the IAEA that the DPRK was compelled to declare its withdrawal from the NPT in March 1993 when a touch-and-go situation was created on the Korean Peninsula.

As it has become clear once again that the US persistently seeks to stifle the DPRK at any cost and the IAEA is used as a tool for executing the US hostile policy towards the DPRK, we can no longer remain bound to the NPT, allowing the country's security and the dignity of our nation to be infringed upon.

North Korea Withdraws from the NPT in Self-Defense

Under the grave situation where our state's supreme interests are most seriously threatened, the DPRK government adopts the following decisions to protect the sovereignty of the country and the nation and their right to existence and dignity: firstly, the DPRK government declares an automatic and immediate effectuation of its withdrawal from the NPT, on which "it unilaterally announced a moratorium as long as it deemed necessary" according to the 11 June, 1993, DPRK-US joint statement, now that the US has unilaterally abandoned its commitments to stop nuclear threat and renounce hostility towards the DPRK in line with the same statement.

Secondly, it declares that the DPRK withdrawing from the NPT is totally free from the binding force of the safeguards accord with the IAEA under its Article 3.

The withdrawal from the NPT is a legitimate self-defensive measure taken against the US moves to stifle the DPRK and the unreasonable behaviour of the IAEA following the US though we pull out of the NPT, we have no intention to produce nuclear weapons and our nuclear activities at this stage will be confined only to peaceful purposes such as the production of electricity.

If the US drops its hostile policy to stifle the DPRK and stops its nuclear threat to the DPRK, the DPRK may prove through a separate verification between the DPRK and the US that it does not make any nuclear weapon.

The United States and the IAEA will never evade their responsibilities for compelling the DPRK to withdraw from the NPT, by ignoring the DPRK's last efforts to seek a peaceful settlement of the nuclear issue through negotiations.

North Korea Poses a Major Nuclear Threat

By Lou Dobbs

As Lou Dobbs, a journalist and CNN anchor, explains in the following article, Kim Jong Il and North Korea's nuclear weapons capability could have a devastating effect on the world. North Korea presents a combination of dangerous factors that could result in an explosion. First, North Korea is suffering from the tyranny of Kim Jong Il and a shattered economy. While his country's economy deteriorates, Kim Jong Il continues to pump resources into building up his military, producing the fifth-largest conventional armed forces in the world, as well as stocks of chemical and biological weapons and ballistic missiles. Worse, North Korea is known to already have at least one nuclear weapon and has announced plans to begin reprocessing nuclear fuel, which will enable it to create enough nuclear material to build five or six additional nuclear bombs.

The global threat posed by these developments includes not only the possibility that North Korea could decide to sell nuclear weapons, given its desperate need for cash, but also the risk that North Korea would have the option of using nuclear weapons offensively for the first time in its history. Preliminary negotiations between North Korea, the United States, and China took place in April 2003, but it may prove difficult to convince North Korea to roll back its nuclear weapons program. If international pressures cannot force North Korea to change its behaviors, military options may be considered.

The crisis on the Korean peninsula is escalating at a frightening speed, even as talks to defuse the crisis have begun, if fitfully. And

Lou Dobbs, "Nuclear Nightmare," *U.S. News & World Report*, May 5, 2003, p. 32. Copyright © 2003 by U.S. News & World Report, Inc. Reproduced by permission of the author.

the threat of the tyrannical Kim Jong Il in North Korea and his nuclear weapons arsenal could have a devastating effect on the geopolitics and economics of that region and, perhaps, the world.

The Dangers of a Nuclear North Korea

An explosive combination of factors is now in play in Pyongyang, including a cruel despot, an economy in ruins, and a nuclear weapons program that North Korean officials have threatened to accelerate. North Korea's per capita gross domestic product was an estimated $1,000 last year.

That's compared with $19,000 in South Korea, which has twice the population of North Korea. As many as 2 million North Koreans are thought to have died from starvation since the mid-'90s. And 42 percent of children in North Korea are chronically malnourished.

But while the North Korean economy implodes, its government continues to pour resources into its military. "North Korea has the fifth-largest standing army in the world with 1.1 million men in arms," says Chung Min Lee, professor at Yonsei University in Seoul. "It has over 700 ballistic missiles that target everything in South Korea and parts of Japan." And we now know that those missiles could reach the West Coast of the United States. Lee adds that North Korea also has a very large stockpile of biological and chemical weapons. North Korea has admitted to having at least one nuclear bomb, senior Bush administration sources have told CNN, and could soon be adding to its nuclear arsenal. Recently, it restarted a plutonium-based nuclear reactor at Yongbyon, which can be used to create the fuel for nuclear bombs. And in the past two weeks [April 21–May 5, 2003], North Korea has acknowledged it is moving forward with plans to reprocess that fuel. Robert Gallucci, former assistant secretary of state in the Clinton administration, says "whether it's in six months or in 12 months," North Korea will have enough material for five or six weapons. . . .

Policy Options and Risks

Compounding the problem, North Korea has already passed significant ballistic missile technology on to Iran, Pakistan, and Syria—a terrifying precedent for a country with nuclear weapons, an economy on the brink, and a starving population. That level of risk is understandably unacceptable to the United States and, we would hope, the world. Last week [April 23–25, 2003], the United States, North Korea, and China met in Beijing for initial talks to resolve the issues. The discussions follow months of wrangling between Washington and Pyongyang over whether the talks should be one on one or multilateral. But even with a preliminary dialogue underway, the options to bring North

Korea back under control are complex and limited. "We can negotiate. We can pressure them. Or we can move to try to make them collapse," says Eric Heginbotham of the Council on Foreign Relations.

"The leverage, obviously, has to be both negative and positive," says former National Security Adviser Zbigniew Brzezinski. "The negative leverage is the threat, for example, of a regional boycott . . . of eventually even a regional embargo on North Korea and, as a last resort, even military action. But to achieve that you have to have a great deal of political consensus, and that's very difficult to manufacture." He adds that the positive inducements are some form of economic assistance but cautions "that may not be enough at this stage to get the North Koreans to roll back what they're already doing. They may be willing to slow down or to stop, but to have them really dismantle what they have been doing is going to take a lot of pressure."

The United States has already cut back our foreign aid, as have Japan and the European Union, according to Nicholas Eberstadt of the American Enterprise Institute. "The other two actors who have to be encouraged are South Korea and China . . . and there's much less political support for aid to North Korea than there was a year ago [2002] in South Korea—and that leaves China as the question mark." And what a big question mark it is. China is North Korea's No. 1 trading partner, and Eberstadt estimates that China provides as much as $470 million in aid to North Korea. If international pressures do not succeed in forcing a change in regime or policies and conduct, says Eberstadt, then "at the end of the road, there are unpleasant military options that would have to be discussed."

Other Concerns

Concerns about conflict in the region are already pressuring regional economies. Debt-rating agency Moody's has downgraded South Korea to "negative"—a move that Heginbotham says "got South Korea to start reexamining their North Korea policy much more than the nuclear crisis itself." Brzezinski says that in the past, North Korea couldn't use nuclear weapons offensively because it would have nothing left. "But once they have several," he warns, "then they are in a much better position to exercise choice, even to exert blackmail."

U.S. Policy Must Respond to North Korea's Intentions

By Phillip C. Saunders

The following selection is excerpted from a magazine article written by Phillip C. Saunders, director of the East Asian Nonproliferation Program at the Center for Nonproliferation Studies, Monterey Institute of International Studies. As Saunders points out, the international community is divided over how to respond to North Korea's 2002 admission that it is again developing nuclear weapons. North Korea's neighbors—China, Russia, and South Korea—believe that a peaceful solution can be obtained if the United States agrees to negotiate directly with North Korea. The United States, however, is reluctant to respond to what it sees as nuclear "blackmail" (in which North Korea makes threats to extort concessions from the United States) and has sought multinational negotiations that would involve South Korea and China.

As Saunders explains, these differing approaches reflect different assessments of North Korea's intentions. These questions of intention are difficult because information about North Korean decision making is not available and North Korea seeks to hide its true intentions to maximize its bargaining power. In this selection Saunders discusses five possible motivations for North Korea's behavior and discusses four options for U.S. policy. He concludes that negotiation with North Korea remains the only viable option for the United States and argues that negotiations can be structured in a way that will test North Korean intentions.

There are growing divisions over how to deal with North Korea's nuclear weapons program. For South Korean political leaders, Washington's unwillingness to negotiate directly with Pyongyang is a barrier to a deal that could resolve the current nuclear crisis peace-

Phillip C. Saunders, "Confronting Ambiguity: How to Handle North Korea's Nuclear Program," *Arms Control Today*, March 2003. Copyright © 2003 by Arms Control Association. Reproduced by permission.

fully—a view that is shared by Russia, China, and Japan. U.S. officials, on the other hand, are skeptical that a negotiated deal would permanently eliminate North Korea's nuclear weapons and missile capabilities, and they believe that pressure and a multilateral dialogue are needed to avoid rewarding North Korea's bad behavior. As President George W. Bush vowed in his State of the Union address, "America and the world will not be blackmailed."

Difficulties in Assessing North Korea's Intentions

These contrasting approaches rest largely on differing assessments of North Korea's objectives. North Korea maintains that it is not out to blackmail anyone, but one of the principal challenges in resolving the current crisis is evaluating Pyongyang's true intentions. Do North Korean leaders view nuclear weapons as a means of forcibly reunifying the Korean Peninsula? Have they decided that nuclear weapons are essential to the regime's survival, making a negotiated deal impossible? Or is the nuclear weapons program a bargaining chip that North Korea is prepared to trade away for the right price? These questions are hard to answer. One problem is that reliable information about the internal dynamics of North Korean decision-making is scarce. A second problem is that North Korean leaders have strong incentives to conceal their true intentions in order to maximize their bargaining power and to minimize international reactions to their nuclear weapons program.

The difficulty of assessing North Korean intentions was demonstrated during the negotiation of the 1994 Agreed Framework, under which North Korea froze its nuclear weapons program in exchange for heavy-fuel oil and two light-water reactors. The Agreed Framework capped North Korea's ability to produce plutonium, but it did not answer the question of whether North Korea already had enough plutonium to make nuclear weapons. A key North Korean objective in the negotiations appeared to be to maintain ambiguity about its nuclear status for as long as possible to maximize its bargaining power. That is why North Korean negotiators rebuffed U.S. demands for immediate special inspections. If inspections revealed that North Korea did not have enough plutonium for nuclear weapons, the United States would take North Korea less seriously, reducing Pyongyang's negotiating leverage. Conversely, if inspections revealed that North Korea already had sufficient plutonium to build weapons, the United States might not agree to a deal. Ultimately, the Agreed Framework required special inspections that would determine North Korea's nuclear history before key components of the two nuclear reactors would be delivered. This compromise allowed North Korea to maintain ambiguity about its nuclear capabilities—and bargaining leverage over the United States—for an additional eight years.

The current crisis began in October 2002, when U.S. officials confronted North Korea with evidence of a uranium-enrichment program, which is a second path to the development of nuclear weapons. North Korean officials reportedly admitted the existence of a nuclear weapons program and began a series of steps to pressure the United States to negotiate with them, despite the U.S. government's insistence that it would not "reward bad behavior" with concessions. As the crisis has escalated, the Bush administration has continued to refuse to negotiate directly with North Korea until it dismantles its uranium-enrichment program. The United States has tried to mobilize international pressure against the North and to find a multilateral forum for talks that would include the major countries in East Asia.

North Korea says it wants U.S. recognition of North Korea's sovereignty, security assurances, and no hindrance of the North's economic development. North Korean officials have stated that, despite their withdrawal from the nuclear Nonproliferation Treaty (NPT), North Korea does not intend to produce nuclear weapons "at this time." But it is still unclear whether the North Korean uranium-enrichment program should be interpreted as evidence that North Korea intended to cheat on the Agreed Framework all along, that it was hedging against the possible collapse of the framework, or that it sought new negotiating leverage once the framework began to erode.

The difficulty of accurately assessing North Korea's nuclear intentions greatly complicates the task of formulating a coordinated and effective policy response. If North Korean leaders are determined to pursue a nuclear weapons capability, then the policy objective must be to find a way to stop them or at least to mitigate the damage North Korean nuclear weapons would do to East Asian security and to the nuclear nonproliferation regime. However, if North Korean leaders are willing to abandon their nuclear weapons program in exchange for security assurances and economic assistance, then the goal should be to craft a verifiable deal that will remove their weapons capability. Disagreements about the motives behind North Korean actions have caused serious splits on Korean policy within the Bush administration and between the United States and its Asian allies and other regional actors such as China and Russia. . . .

Possible Intentions of North Korea

Five scenarios should be considered in assessing North Korea's nuclear intentions:

1. North Korean leaders have decided that nuclear weapons are essential to their security.

This scenario argues that North Korean leaders feel threatened by superior U.S. military capabilities and by U.S. talk about regime change and pre-emptive strikes. North Korean leaders may have concluded that nuclear weapons are the only way to guarantee regime survival in the face of such threats. (This scenario is consistent with U.S. intelligence assessments that North Korea produced one or two nuclear weapons in the mid- to late 1990s.)

If this is the case, there is probably no peaceful settlement that can stop or roll back the North Korean nuclear weapons program unless North Korean leaders change their minds. The United States, South Korea, Japan, and China must either take military action to destroy North Korean nuclear facilities and stockpiles or learn to live with North Korean nuclear weapons by relying on deterrence and missile defenses. North Korea's pursuit of multiple pathways to nuclear weapons and efforts to develop long-range ballistic missiles indicates that the regime has devoted considerable resources to developing deliverable nuclear weapons.

On the other hand, North Korea has passed up a number of opportunities to accelerate its nuclear and missile programs. If North Korea had not signed the Agreed Framework, it could have continued operation of its research reactor, completed construction on its 50-megawatt and 200-megawatt reactors, and reprocessed the spent fuel to produce plutonium. By now, the regime could have had enough fissile material for at least 150–200 nuclear weapons. North Korea also declared a unilateral moratorium on flight tests of long-range missiles. This restraint appears inconsistent with a decision that operational, deliverable nuclear weapons are essential for North Korean security—unless North Korean leaders feel that one or two nuclear weapons are enough to deter a U.S. attack.

2. North Korean leaders are willing to negotiate their nuclear and missile programs away for a deal that guarantees their security and sovereignty.

This scenario argues that North Korean leaders feel threatened by superior U.S. military capabilities and by U.S. efforts to keep the North Korean regime isolated economically and politically. North Korea has pursued nuclear weapons and ballistic missiles to create the leverage necessary to build a new relationship with the United States that will ensure the regime's survival and create a better environment for economic reforms.

Evidence for this scenario includes repeated statements by North Korean leaders about their willingness to negotiate deals with the

United States to restrict their nuclear and missile capabilities and to curb missile exports. The Agreed Framework, the missile flight-test moratorium, and talks with the Clinton administration about a missile deal are indicators of North Korea's willingness to limit its military capabilities.

From this perspective, North Korea's efforts to develop a highly enriched uranium capability are attempts to develop a new bargaining chip to trade for economic and security concessions. It is even possible that these efforts were intended to be discovered by the United States in order to be bargained away. (North Korea's previous success in persuading the United States to increase food aid in exchange for inspecting a suspect nuclear facility at Kumchang-ri—which turned out to have no nuclear equipment—suggests that a nuclear bluff is a possibility.)

On the other hand, the United States, Japan, South Korea, and China would all like to see North Korea pursue significant economic and political reforms. The door to better relations that would support North Korean economic reforms is wide open, but North Korea has been reluctant to walk through it. Security threats are arguably unnecessary to achieve better relations and may in fact undercut efforts to improve relations and prospects for economic cooperation. (North Korea's demonstrated willingness to cheat on international agreements would also make a future deal very difficult to negotiate because of the damage done to U.S. trust.)

3. North Korean leaders want both nuclear weapons (as an ultimate security guarantee) and better relations with the United States, Japan, and South Korea.

Under this scenario, North Korean leaders have sought to keep their options open by pursuing nuclear and missile programs while simultaneously seeking better relations with the United States, Japan, and South Korea. One possibility is that North Korean leaders view their nuclear and missile programs as a hedge in case they are unable to negotiate a lasting agreement with the United States that will assure the security of their regime. If the United States puts an offer on the table that will guarantee regime survival, then North Korea would be willing to give up its nuclear and missile programs. If the United States does not deliver an acceptable deal, then North Korea will proceed to develop an operational force of missiles armed with nuclear weapons.

Another possibility is that North Korean leaders planned to cheat all along. Agreements to restrict nuclear and missile programs and exports were intended to gain monetary benefits and to buy time until North Korea could develop an operational nuclear weapons capability. Alternatively, North Korean leaders may believe that the United States,

Japan, and South Korea are willing to overlook a small, ambiguous North Korean nuclear weapons capability and improve relations anyway. South Korea's "sunshine policy" and Japan's recent efforts to move toward normalization of diplomatic relations despite concerns about North Korean missiles provide some support for this belief.

Both the hedge scenario and the cheat scenario explain some aspects of North Korea's behavior, such as the relatively small scale of its nuclear weapons program, its willingness to accept temporary limits on the size of its nuclear arsenal (while pursuing efforts to develop more advanced capabilities), and its eagerness to reach out to the United States, Japan, and (to a lesser extent) South Korea. These scenarios suggest that North Korean leaders either miscalculated the negative international response to their nuclear brinkmanship and cheating or feel that the negative consequences can be overcome once an agreement is in place.

4. North Korean leaders/factions disagree about whether nuclear weapons or a negotiated agreement with the United States is the best way to achieve security.

This scenario views inconsistent North Korean behavior as the product of the shifting strength of different domestic political factions. One faction, centered on the military, may feel that nuclear weapons are essential to North Korean security; another may feel that a negotiated agreement offers more security. Each faction has some ability to undertake international actions independently of the other.

This scenario could explain why North Korea sometimes acts cooperatively to seek agreements and sometimes behaves in a bellicose manner to undercut negotiations. It also offers a potential explanation for why North Korea has pursued a uranium-enrichment program. As some of the promised benefits of the Agreed Framework (such as provision of the reactors and progress toward normalization of relations with the United States) were delayed, the balance of power in Pyongyang may have shifted away from engagement and toward efforts to develop nuclear weapons to ensure North Korea's security. (Alternatively, earlier North Korean efforts to acquire uranium-enrichment technology and production equipment from Pakistan would suggest a decision to cheat on the Agreed Framework or to hedge against the possibility of its collapse.)

Although this explanation can explain uncoordinated and inconsistent North Korean behavior, North Korea's negotiating style sometimes emphasizes careful efforts to control the atmospherics of a negotiation and to maximize pressure on a negotiating partner through carefully coordinated actions and statements. This kind of control is difficult to explain with a factional model. It is also important to note that dealing with a changing balance of power between factions in Pyongyang could make it hard (or impossible) to get a negotiated deal that would last.

5. North Korean leaders seek nuclear weapons and ballistic missiles to enable offensive actions against South Korea.

The preceding scenarios all assume that the primary objective for North Korean leaders is defensive: ensuring the survival of the current regime. An alternative assumption is that North Korean leaders view nuclear weapons as a useful offensive tool for achieving their long-stated objective of unification on their own terms. The U.S. military alliance with South Korea is one of the main obstacles to forced reunification. This scenario emphasizes the potential value of nuclear weapons and long-range missiles that can hold U.S. territory at risk in order to prevent the United States from intervening in response to a North Korean invasion or military coercion of the South. This scenario has been raised repeatedly by missile defense advocates, who argue that a rogue state might use a nuclear-armed missile capability to deter the United States from intervening in a conflict. U.S. freedom of action, they say, could be maintained only through missile defenses.

This scenario is consistent with other aspects of North Korea's military doctrine and force deployments. Most North Korean military units are located close to the demilitarized zone and are positioned and trained to undertake offensive operations. North Korean chemical and biological weapons capabilities, massive artillery bombardments, and special operations forces could be used to support an invasion of the South. From this perspective, North Korea's professed interest in negotiating an agreement to give up its missile and nuclear capabilities might be intended to mask its efforts to acquire useable capabilities. Alternatively, North Korea may hope to drive wedges between South Korea and the United States that weaken or dissolve their alliance. (South Korean statements that Seoul should play the role of "mediator" between Pyongyang and Washington suggest that a wedge strategy might be having some success.)

The difficulty with this argument is that North Korea's ability to mount a successful invasion of the South has eroded as its economy has imploded. South Korea has continued to modernize its military and improve its training, while North Korea has not imported major new weapons systems in more than a decade. The North Korean military suffers from shortages of spare parts for its imported weapons systems, and limited supplies of fuel have impeded training. If North Korea's objective was to invade the South, it would probably have made efforts to acquire nuclear weapons and long-range missiles much more quickly, rather than freezing key elements of its plutonium production capability and issuing a unilateral freeze on missile flight testing. Although this scenario cannot be ruled out, the principal "evidence" for it is that a nuclear-weapon capability could theoretically deter the United States.

Dealing with Uncertainty

Each of these five scenarios explains some aspects of North Korean behavior. Unfortunately, it is hard to tell which is correct. If nuclear weapons are intended to enable offensive military options, then North Korean officials are likely to use deceptive measures to hide their intentions. If they have decided that nuclear weapons are necessary for their survival, then creating the impression that U.S. aggression forced them into a weapons program may improve their international image. (North Korea has had some success in persuading Asian governments that U.S. intransigence is largely to blame for the current crisis.) On the other hand, even if North Korea is prepared to negotiate away its nuclear weapons capabilities, it still has incentives to appear reluctant and bellicose—even unpredictable—in order to strike the best possible bargain.

U.S. policymakers have tried to devise policy approaches that address the difficulty of judging North Korean intentions. The policy review conducted by former Secretary of Defense William Perry in 1998 and 1999 called for a two-path strategy in order to test North Korean intentions. Perry recommended offering North Korea a choice between the alternatives of deeper engagement and improved relations with the United States or continued hostility and enhanced containment. "By incorporating two paths, the strategy devised in the review avoids any dependence on conjectures regarding [North Korean] intentions or behavior and neither seeks, nor depends upon for its success, a transformation of [North Korea's] internal system." The difficulty with this approach is that the key criterion for judging whether or not North Korea is following the path of engagement—Pyongyang's willingness to give up its weapons of mass destruction programs in a verifiable way—requires North Korea to give up its most important piece of negotiating leverage at the beginning of the process.

The Agreed Framework attempted to work around this problem by structuring the agreement as a series of reciprocal steps that would eventually produce transparency about North Korea's nuclear history. However, delays in reactor construction and the erosion of political support for the Agreed Framework in the United States meant that important aspects of the agreement, such as improved U.S. economic and political relations with North Korea, were not fully implemented. The Perry policy review envisioned a similar "step-by-step and reciprocal" process as a means of surmounting this problem, but this approach was never fully put into practice.

Determining U.S. Policy

The United States needs to approach the current crisis with a strategy that acknowledges its inability to know North Korean intentions. Given that any of the five scenarios above could be correct, U.S. strategy should seek to test North Korean intentions without compromising U.S. security interests. At this stage in the crisis, the United States basically has four options: using military force to attack North Korea's nuclear infrastructure, mobilizing international pressure against North Korea, waiting North Korea out, and negotiating. Military strikes appear to have been ruled out because of their inability to destroy any current North Korean nuclear weapons or plutonium stocks, strong opposition from U.S. allies and other countries in the region, and North Korea's ability to retaliate and cause severe damage to South Korea. . . .

If no agreement is reached, North Korea is likely to reprocess its spent fuel rods and acquire sufficient plutonium for another four to six nuclear weapons. Once the reprocessing is complete (in four to six months), the United States would lose the option of military strikes against this material. With sufficient material for five to eight nuclear weapons, North Korea would have new options, including nuclear testing, possible operational deployment of nuclear weapons, and selling weapons-grade fissile material. Moreover, North Korean leaders are highly unlikely to wait passively for international pressure or domestic economic problems to cause their regime to collapse. Instead, they would use provocative actions to escalate the crisis in order to increase the pressure on the United States to make a deal. . . .

It makes sense to explore whether a negotiated deal is possible. Regardless of the ultimate outcome, negotiations would have some immediate political value. First, the United States should insist on a verifiable freeze on North Korean reprocessing activity during negotiations. This would halt North Korea's movement toward an increased nuclear weapons capability and buy time. In return, the United States would pledge not to attack North Korea during the negotiations, a concession that the Bush administration has already offered without getting anything in return. Second, negotiations would ease growing splits between the United States and its allies, making it easier to forge a united policy toward North Korea. If negotiations failed to reach an acceptable and verifiable agreement, the United States would be better positioned to win international support for a tougher approach. Third, negotiations would reduce North Korea's ability to escalate the crisis, allowing the United States to seize the initiative and focus attention on North Korean weapons of mass destruction and ways of verifying an agreement. They would also reduce the possibility of a North Korean military provocation in the midst of a war in Iraq. On balance, negotiations hold more promise for achieving the goal of a nuclear-weapons free Korean Peninsula.

Negotiating an acceptable agreement will not be easy. The fact that North Korea violated the Agreed Framework and its other nuclear non-proliferation commitments means that the United States and other parties to a possible new agreement will require stringent measures to verify North Korean compliance. But paradoxically, domestic suspicion of North Korean intentions may make it easier for U.S. negotiators to insist upon strong verification measures as a necessary condition for an agreement. This is especially true if congressional support is needed to finance an agreement. It will be difficult to craft a verifiable agreement that can test North Korean intentions. But even if negotiations fail, the United States will be in a better position for having tried.

Negotiation with North Korea Is Doomed to Failure

By Bok Ku Lee

The following selection is written by a North Korean defector who worked in Kim Il Sung's weapons of mass destruction program. Bok Ku Lee *is a pseudonym used by the author to protect the safety of his family. In his article, published by the* Wall Street Journal, *Lee explains that he worked as head of the technical department at a North Korean missile munitions plant, part of the country's weapons of mass destruction industry. He describes his escape from North Korea and his defection to South Korea as well as South Korea's disinterest in his testimony about weapons of mass destruction or North Korean atrocities. South Korean officials, he claims, did not want him to speak out because they feared his testimony might jeopardize their policy of engagement toward North Korea. In 2002 Lee was able to travel to the United States, where he testified before the Senate. Lee urged the United States to avoid entering into agreements with North Korea that provide the regime with assistance in return for guarantees to discontinue its weapons of mass destruction programs. Such agreements, Lee argued, will fail because any help given to the regime only strengthens the regime and supports its determination to develop such weapons.*

Bok Ku Lee is not my real name, but one I've adopted to protect my family.

For a number of years I served as head of the technical department at a munitions complex that made missile guidance systems and related electronic devices for North Korea's military. I was one of 100,000 or so scientific and professional people involved in the regime's weapons of mass destruction industry.

Bok Ku Lee, "A Defector's Story," *Wall Street Journal*, June 5, 2003. Copyright © 2003 by Dow Jones & Company, Inc. Reproduced by permission.

While I made enough money to modestly feed my family, I witnessed mass starvation and oppression of those less fortunate, and unspeakable abuses of power and lifestyle excesses by senior political officials of the regime. As did everyone, I lived in constant fear of being sent to the gulag for the slightest indiscretion.

Nonetheless, I was trusted with some of the regime's biggest secrets. While serving, I was sent to Iran to test launch one of our missiles with a new guidance system for the then-ruling Ayatollah Khomeini. I consulted with colleagues who were sent to serve on an operational war basis for Saddam Hussein during the first Gulf War, and others who were sent to other countries to sell, service and install such missile systems. I ordered, supervised and monitored the foreign purchases of electronic and guidance material—90% of which came from Japanese suppliers. I worked with some of the 60 or so Russian scientists who had been "cherry picked" by the regime to work in Pyongyang's nuclear, atomic, chemical and biological warfare programs—and who continue to work there.

Escape to South Korea

Yet, like most of my fellow countrymen, I longed for the day when I could escape the Stalinist prison my country had become. That day came six years ago. I made my escape in July 1997 by crossing the Yalu River into China after sundown. I lived in China for two years with enough money, contacts and employable skills to make me less vulnerable to starvation or capture than most North Korean refugees. That said, I lived in constant terror of capture by Chinese authorities, for I knew that such capture would have resulted in a death sentence upon repatriation to the North. In 1999, thanks to an ethnic Korean in China who notified me of a fishing boat scheduled to ferry dozens of illegal laborers that very night, and, unknown to the operators of this boat, I escaped to South Korea as a true stowaway.

Upon my arrival, I was debriefed by South Korea's National Intelligence Service, and occasionally put in the hands of unsophisticated American questioners in Seoul. Remarkably, the South Korean officials made it clear to me that I would be in danger if I were to speak out about the WMD programs I had worked on or the atrocities I had witnessed. It soon became obvious that they feared my testimony because it might jeopardize South Korea's "sunshine policy," which seeks to keep the North's repressive regime in power in order to avoid the economic consequences to the South were it to collapse.

Incredibly, Seoul seems unwilling to accept that propping up Kim Jong Il's regime has had grave consequences for the world. While traveling to the China–North Korea border last year [2002] I met with former colleagues and learned that the production at our old missile guidance system plant was up to normal levels following receipt by the regime of substantial amounts of foreign currency from the South. In 1997, when I left the plant, the output had shriveled to 30% of the pre-Nodong One launch in 1993 due to the lack of hard currency that had limited the capacity to pay for Japanese parts imports.

Witness Against North Korea

Last year [2002] facing increased pressures from the South Korean Intelligence Service to remain an invisible man, I decided to do all I could to escape from South Korea's hands. I obtained a passport under the pretense of traveling to Japan, and, with the aid of an underground-railroad activist, obtained a visa that brought me to the U.S. While here, I put on a hood to protect my identity, held a press conference in Washington and testified before the Senate in open and closed sessions about what I know about Pyongyang's weapons of mass destruction.

The reaction to my activities on the part of the South Korean intelligence was immediate. My wife, a North Korean escapee who'd been captured by the Chinese and sent to a North Korean prison before escaping again, was subjected to threatening phone calls from police and intelligence officials that so terrorized her as to cause her collapse and hospitalization. Thanks to the intervention of Senators Richard Lugar, Peter Fitzgerald and Daniel Akaka—to whom I shall remain forever grateful—South Korean officials have since been contacted about the treatment of my wife, and the harassment and intimidation have, for the moment, ceased.

Advice to America

My experience as a North Korean weapons official and defector, and my knowledge and ongoing relations with other defectors and current North Korean officials, led me to a few critical conclusions that may be of value to American officials who now, in a post-Iraq world, are confronting full-force the reality of Pyongyang's [North Korea's capital] lunatic regime.

First, "understandings" with Pyongyang that cause the exchange of hard currency for "guarantees" that the regime will discontinue its nuclear and WMD [weapons of mass destruction] programs are both immoral and doomed to failure. Immoral because such understandings come, in the end, to this: promises by Pyongyang not to export terrorism are exchanged for assurances to Pyongyang that it is licensed to commit as much terrorism against its own people as it wishes. And doomed to failure because, as the Clinton agreements [reference to 1994 agreement in which North Korea agreed not to develop nuclear weapons in exchange for two light-water reactors and fuel] prove, any effort to finance, legitimize or empower the regime only strengthens its desire and capacity to develop weapons of mass destruction.

I come from a country whose rulers are indifferent to the mass starvation of their own people—one whose citizens are on average more than seven inches shorter than their Southern brothers and sisters, and one that requires its citizens to rise early in the morning to join screeching public-address systems in singing absurd songs of praise to a deranged leader. But—and this is now increasingly true and true to a degree that would have seemed impossible 10 years ago—my fellow countrymen know *and openly acknowledge* that Kim Jong Il is both evil and lunatic *and doomed.* More and more, midlevel officials like me in the North Korean military and WMD industry see the regime's blustering threats against other countries as evidence of its isolation, desperation and declining hold on power.

The time has come for South Korea and the U.S. to encourage the defection of thousands like me who are prepared to tell the world what they know and whose departure will deprive the regime of skills it needs to survive. Such mass defections *will* occur if the defectors are given a reasonable prospect for safe harbor outside of North Korea. At the same time, Seoul should end its barbarous "sunshine policy," which sentences fellow Koreans to slavery because giving them freedom would cost too much money.

In short, the time has come to recognize that a policy of promoting democracy, insisting and ensuring that humanitarian aid actually go to the hungry rather than the regime, and encouraging mass defections, will cause the repeat in North Korea of what happened when East Germans defected to Austria through Hungary, thereby triggering the implosion of the Soviet Union without a shot being fired. This is a real and likely prospect for the oppressed people of my country and for world security.

CHAPTER 3

North Korean Instability and the Asian-Pacific Region

North Korea's Weapons of Mass Destruction Threaten South Korea

By Bruce Bennett

The following article by Bruce Bennett discusses the threat North Korea's nuclear weapons pose to South Korea. Bennett notes that many South Koreans do not fear attack by North Korea despite the hostility that has existed between the two Koreas since the Korean War. The reality, however, is that South Korea has much to fear from North Korea, which is armed with weapons of mass destruction, including nuclear weapons, and has a strategy for using them against South Korea.

North Korea's strategy, Bennett claims, is to use weapons of mass destruction to catastrophically damage South Korean and U.S. military forces so that it can then use its outdated conventional military effectively. Specifically, North Korea plans to use artillery with chemical weapons against South Korean and U.S. forces on the battlefield, long-range artillery and chemical/ biological weapons against Seoul and ground forces positioned behind the battlefield, and ballistic missiles armed with chemical and possibly nuclear weapons for rear or off-peninsula targets. Bennett says that North Korea's intent, which it states often, is to conquer South Korea; believing anything else, he says, is folly. Bruce Bennett is a senior policy analyst at RAND, a nonprofit research and analysis institution.

Bruce Bennett, "North Korea's Threat to South Korea," United Press International, March 7, 2003. Copyright © 2003 by United Press International. Reproduced by permission.

In 1915, 50 years after the last shots were fired in the American Civil War, few people could imagine the resumption of hostilities between the North and South. Today, almost 50 years after the end of the civil war between North and South Korea, growing numbers of young people in the South similarly can't imagine a new war with their "brothers and sisters" in the North.

But while America's Civil War ended with the preservation of the United States, Korea's led only to an angry armistice between two hostile states facing each other at gunpoint. Despite this, for growing numbers of South Koreans, the 400,000 deaths their nation suffered at the hands of their northern brethren in the 1950s are merely words in history books. This is why many young South Koreans today seem convinced that an attack from North Korea is extraordinarily unlikely.

This belief is at odds with reality: Even though it has the 13th largest economy in the world and a strong military, South Korea has much to fear from its dangerous northern neighbor, which is armed with weapons of mass destruction—probably including nuclear weapons—and which, even more frighteningly, has developed a specific strategy for using them.

North Korea's Weapons of Mass Destruction Strategy

Some military experts say the North Korean military is far inferior to South Korean and American forces, and therefore is not a serious threat. They rightly note that while North Korea has a military force of more than 1 million, most of its conventional weapons and equipment were designed in the 1950s and 1960s—making them old, hard to maintain and prone to breakdowns.

But far from being a reason to relax, this situation may in fact be the foundation for the current grave threat against South Korea. It was the basis, say some of these same experts, for a decision made about 20 years ago by North Korea that it could not compete with the modernizing South Korean and U.S. military forces, and that it would instead emphasize weapons of mass destruction.

According to these experts, North Korea seems to have opted for a three-tiered strategy that involves using weapons of mass destruction to catastrophically damage South Korean and U.S. forces to the point where the outdated North Korean equipment and weapons might still be effective.

The strategy's components are as follows:

—Against South Korean and American battlefield forces, North Korea has emphasized artillery with chemical weapons, and built a huge arsenal of each.

—Against the nearby South Korean capital Seoul and ground force reserves behind the battlefield, North Korea has emphasized long-range artillery with chemical weapons, and special forces with biological weapons.

—Against rear area and off-peninsula targets, North Korea has emphasized ballistic missiles with chemical weapons and special forces with biological weapons, and the development of nuclear weapons.

Possible Damage to South Korea

The North Koreans could cause tremendous damage whether or not this strategy works. For example, one battery of North Korean 240-mm multiple rocket launchers fired into Seoul can deliver roughly a ton of chemical weapons, which, according to various accounts, could kill or injure thousands or tens of thousands. North Korea has many such batteries.

In addition, North Korean special forces teams might each spray several kilograms of anthrax in Seoul, leaving tens to hundreds of thousands of people infected, many of whom would die unless properly treated.

A North Korean nuclear weapon fired into Seoul might cause damage similar to that of the nuclear weapon detonated on Hiroshima in World War II, which left some 70,000 dead and 75,000 injured.

It is generally believed that if North Korea has only one or two nuclear weapons, the regime will likely withhold them unless it faces certain defeat and destruction. But if it builds five or 10 nuclear weapons, as it may soon do, it may be inclined to use some against South Korea early in the conflict to demonstrate its power and rapidly achieve some military objectives. It might also sell some of these weapons to terrorists who could try to use them against the United States or its allies.

Reunification Unlikely If North Korean Threat Continues

The end of the American Civil War reunified the United States and ended a terrible crisis for our country. In contrast, the armed, fragile, jittery 50-year hiatus in the civil war between the two Koreas has yielded the opposite. It has created a modern, prosperous, ever-evolving state in the south—a valuable member of the world economic community—and a totalitarian, aggressive, and dangerous nation in the north, whose only source of power on the world stage has been to create as many threats as it can to the peace and security of the region, and then push them as far as possible in order to attract attention and exact concessions.

North Korea is a police state led by a dictator who has a specific strategy—and an often-stated intent—to conquer South Korea. Believing anything else is an illusion, and the latest generation of South Koreans does that at their peril—and at the peril of the other nations in Northeast Asia, which would all suffer from such a war.

While this grave risk might be healed by the eventual peaceful reunification of the two Koreas, it is unlikely that will happen as long as Kim Jong Il's [leader of North Korea] preferred method of "diplomacy" involves threatening South Korea and some of his other neighbors with weapons of mass destruction.

A Nuclear North Korea Could Lead to an Arms Race in Asia

By Thomas Omestad, Mark Mazzetti, Jennifer Hanawald, and Roger Du Mars

This selection is excerpted from an article published in U.S. News & World Report *and written by four journalists—Thomas Omestad, Mark Mazzetti, Jennifer Hanawald, and Roger Du Mars. The article describes U.S. concerns about the effects of a nuclearization of North Korea. Foremost among these concerns is that it might spur an Asian arms race in which North Korea's neighbors decide to increase their military readiness by obtaining nuclear weapons and missiles to respond to the North Korean threat. This possibility, the authors say, is what makes many policy makers see the North Korea nuclear crisis as a major threat to global security.*

Some analysts are worried that North Korea has simply decided to build up its nuclear arsenal to deter a U.S. attack. If North Korea restarts its nuclear reprocessing plant, it could produce six to seven nuclear bombs within a few months. This could provide North Korea's leader, Kim Jong Il, with various options, including selling nuclear weapons. The key to resolving the crisis, the article suggests, is China, North Korea's main economic supporter and thus the country that has the most influence with North Korea.

It is a scenario that some U.S. officials find too sensitive to discuss in detail: A defiant North Korea chooses to build and keep a nuclear arsenal, not bargain it away for rewards, as many suppose. Faced with a nuclear breakout by a hostile regime, Japan reconsiders its antinu-

Thomas Omestad, Mark Mazzetti, Jennifer Hanawald, and Roger Du Mars, "A Balance of Terror," U.S. News & World Report, January 27, 2003. Copyright © 2003 by U.S. News & World Report, Inc. Reproduced by permission.

clear taboos, fields a larger missile force of its own, and plunges into developing a shield against incoming missiles with the United States. South Korea, with one eye on the North and the other on Japan, follows suit. China reacts with more nukes and missiles of its own. Taiwan, outgunned, opts for more missiles and, perhaps, nuclear bombs. A nervous Russia shifts nuclear and conventional forces for defense against its old rivals, China and Japan, India, a foe of China, expands its nuclear forces, a step that causes Pakistan to do likewise. An Asian arms race snaps into high gear. No wonder that one former U.S. official who helped guide North Korea policy warns of a new "domino effect" in Asia.

Such possibilities—even if only partially realized—are driving some U.S. officials and Asia specialists to conclude that Pyongyang's [North Korea's capital city] nuclear gambit could be the most serious threat to global stability today. In just over three months, North Korea has admitted running a covert program to enrich uranium for bombs, vowed to keep it going, and bustled through measures to prepare for extracting weapons-grade plutonium at another site. What's more, it became the first nation to abandon the Nuclear Nonproliferation Treaty—and declared that it would cast off a moratorium on test-firing ballistic missiles.

Kim Jong Il's Intentions

That may not be an idle threat. A senior State Department official predicted that the North may soon test-fire a long-range missile over Japan, as it did in 1998. The dizzying pace of North Korea's brinkmanship is deepening suspicions that its leader, Kim Jong Il, has made the strategic choice to build a nuclear arsenal in order to deter any potential U.S. attack. Says Victor Cha, a North Korea expert at Georgetown University, "If you're simply trying to create a crisis, you don't need to do all these things.". . .

Kim's actions, note U.S. officials, seem designed to expand his options. He could build up a nuclear arsenal in a bid to win greater concessions through security guarantees, aid, and diplomatic recognition. Or he could keep it as a deterrent force. He might try to do both by hiding a portion of any newly produced fissile material. And having seen India and Pakistan ride out sanctions after their 1998 nuclear tests, Kim may be calculating that he can do likewise. . . .

The North could begin lifting some of the 8,000 plutonium fuel rods from a cooling pool at the Yongbyon reactor complex for reprocessing. That could yield enough weapons-grade plutonium for five to seven bombs by this summer [2003]—on top of the one or two nuclear devices the North may have already. By then, the North would be in a position to consider a dramatic act of brinkmanship: a nuclear test blast. Says a high-ranking State Department official, "If they test and reprocess furiously, it's a monumental change. Everyone in the region has to reassess their defenses."

Some Russian and Chinese military analysts doubt that the North Koreans have been able to make workable weapons. U.S. proliferation specialists, however, believe that the North has conducted dozens of test explosions of the sort that can touch off a chain reaction in plutonium....

A half-dozen nukes would make Asia a different place. "It's a much more threatening capability," says Robert Einhorn, a former top U.S. nonproliferation official. The weapons could be dispersed—and hidden in underground bunkers. And North Korea's track record of selling missiles to countries such as Pakistan and Yemen raises an even more chilling prospect: the world's first department store for nukes, with terrorists and rogue states as potential hard-currency customers. One senior U.S. official doubts Kim would go that far: "I think he knows we would cause him to disappear."

The Response of the United States and Asia

The Bush administration has been trying to orchestrate international pressure on the North to disarm—with limited success. In a shift [in January 2003], the president softened his rhetoric, hinting that impoverished North Korea might receive aid, energy supplies, and even agreements on security and diplomatic recognition if it verifiably quits its nuclear projects. South Korea's incoming president, Roh Moo Hyun, has frustrated administration hawks by portraying himself as a possible mediator between Pyongyang and Washington, and Seoul opposes sanctions or other efforts to isolate the North. Russia, which has friendly ties with the North, remains stuck in a "denial phase" on Pyongyang's nuclear ambitions, says Alexander Vershbow, the U.S. ambassador to Moscow.

China may be the key: North Korea depends on China for food and fuel, but Beijing has been reluctant to squeeze Pyongyang, fearing chaos, mass refugee flows, and a U.S. presence on its border if the North collapses. U.S. officials welcomed China's offer . . . to host U.S.–North Korean talks, but they hope for more. Envoys are reminding the Chinese that Washington has opposed a nuclear-armed Japan or South Korea. "We say, 'We've carried your water on nuclear issues for 50 years. Now it's your turn to do it for us,'" says a senior U.S. diplomat.

Japan has edged closer to the U.S. approach than has South Korea. The Japanese public was enraged by revelations last fall [2002] of North Korean abductions of Japanese. Normalization talks have stalled. After the nuclear crisis emerged, officials in Tokyo approached the Bush administration about increasing Japan's role in theater missile defenses. The revulsion at atomic weapons is deep in Japan, the only country to have suffered a nuclear attack. But the idea that Japan someday might have to abandon its non-nuclear stance has also gained currency in conservative circles. If Pyongyang brandishes atomic weapons, says Ryukichi Imai, a former diplomat and government adviser on atomic energy, "there would be a lot of voices in Japan saying this country should do it too." But, he predicts, "Japan will never have the bomb. We know too much about nuclear weapons." Still, U.S. officials note that Japan has plenty of plutonium and technical knowhow. "Japan in six to 12 months could be missiled and weaponed up," says a senior U.S. official. . . .

South Korea has also shunned the bomb, though it conducted covert nuclear weapons research in the 1970s until the United States leaned on Seoul to shut it down. "They were close," says the U.S. official. "The plans are on the shelf." (Washington also demanded that Taiwan halt its nuclear research around the same time.) Though analysts believe the South might react to a prolonged nuclear crisis by acquiring antimissile systems and perhaps offensive missiles, the Seoul government insists the nuclear question is closed. "South Korea knows it can be safely protected behind the U.S. military. The U.S. [nuclear] umbrella is sufficient," says a senior official in Seoul.

South Korea is also defended by a "tripwire" 37,000-member U.S. military force. Yet even before the current tensions, *U.S. News* has learned, the Pentagon was studying a possible reduction in the ground force, which has been a magnet for anti-American protests in the South, coupled with other changes including greater emphasis on Navy and Air Force precision-strike weapons. Those moves, however, could be complicated by the nuclear crisis if U.S. officials believe that North Korea would interpret them as a weakening of the U.S. commitment to defending the South.

But in Seoul, some people already believe that American nuclear protection isn't enough. "If South Korea has nuclear weapons, then South Korea will never fear North Korea, because it will know that if North Korea bombs South Korea, it will be bombed by us," reasons Kim Young Tak, a 43-year-old middle school teacher. Nuclear deterrence, it's been said, has an undeniable logic.

North Korean Actions Could Cause Japan to Reconsider Pacifism

By Alex Kerr

Alex Kerr is an American author who lives in Japan and has written books on the subject of Japan and Japanese history. Here, Kerr describes how Japan, after its defeat in World War II, enacted a new constitution that embraced pacifism by renouncing war and abandoning the country's right to maintain military forces. This pacifist policy, however, was short-lived as Japan quickly rearmed, with U.S. encouragement. Japan monetarily supported the first Gulf War in 1991 and later in the 1990s sent peacekeeping troops to Cambodia and Afghanistan. Today, Japan is again a great military power, ranking fourth in the world in military expenditures. In fact, Japan has the material and technology to produce nuclear weapons in just a few months' time.

Japan has begun to consider using military force against North Korea if that country continues menacing actions toward Japan, such as its 1998 firing of a ballistic missile over Japan and its 2002 resumption of nuclear weapons production. Indeed, Japan has already signaled its intent to engage North Korea militarily. For example, in 2001 Japan sank a North Korean spy ship. In 2002 Japan's deputy chief cabinet secretary argued that Japan should have nuclear weapons and intercontinental ballistic missiles. In 2003 Japan's defense agency director warned that Japan would use military force against North Korea. Yet to many Japanese, the suggestions that Japan will respond militarily seem shocking given Japan's historical pacifist psychology and the memories of the Hiroshima and Nagasaki nuclear disasters.

Alex Kerr, "A War-Torn Land: Will North Korean Nukes Rouse Japan from Its 'Stupor of Peace'?" *Time International*, vol. 161, February 24, 2003, p. 22. Copyright © 2003 by Time, Inc. Reproduced by permission.

Once upon a time, there was an end to war. In 1929 when the French and Americans were on better terms than they are today, the two nations sponsored a radical new idea: the Kellogg-Briand Pact. Its 62 signatories, which included Russia, the U.S., Japan, China, and most of Europe, agreed to renounce war as a tool of national policy. For about a year it seemed to work. Whereupon, in 1931, Japan invaded Manchuria; in 1935, the Italians attacked Ethiopia and in 1938, Germany occupied Austria, heralding a drive for global dominance that would soon plunge the world back into war.

The Pact evaporated, but it lived on in the mind of one man: General MacArthur. In 1945, at the end of World War II, he wrote the pact's provisions into Article 9 of Japan's new constitution. It decreed that the Japanese people would "forever renounce war as a sovereign right of the nation" and would abandon their right to maintain "land, sea, and air forces, as well as other war potential."

"An ill-fitting suit of clothes," one Japanese politician called it. Yet the people of Japan took pride in Article 9, cherishing it as a real contribution to world peace that had grown out of their devastating defeat. Almost immediately the General regretted it. In 1947 America began pushing Japan to rearm, and by the time the Korean War broke out in 1952, the process was more or less complete. Japan called its military "Self-Defense Forces" to get around Article 9, and today Japan is once again a great military power. With $40.4 billion in annual military expenditure, Japan ranks fourth in the world.

Meanwhile, starting in the 1990s, Japan made a series of small but critical steps to assert itself abroad. At first, Japan only provided money for the Gulf War; then it sent peacekeeping forces to Cambodia and Afghanistan; finally, in 2001, it sank a North Korean spy ship. The debate over whether Japan should rearm is moot: Japan has long since rearmed and is capable of striking far beyond its borders. Indeed, Japan has enough plutonium and the technology to produce nuclear weapons in a matter of months.

And yet, nearly 60 years after World War II ended, Japan is still strapped tightly into the ill-fitting suit of official pacifism. Hence the surprise when Defense Agency director General Shigeru Ishiba declared on Feb. 13 [2003] that Japan would "use military force as a self-defense measure if [North Korea] starts to resort to arms against Japan." In the last few years North Korea has steadily increased its menace, firing a ballistic missile over Japan in 1998, and reigniting its nuclear program early this year [2003]. Yet Ishiba's words still shock because war is, quite simply, against the constitution.

Not that it should matter. Article 9 has been so diluted by doublespeak as to become virtually meaningless. An early strike against Korea, Ishiba explains, would be "defensive," not "pre-emptive." Likewise, in May 2002, Deputy Chief Cabinet Secretary Shinzo Abe declared that Japan could have nuclear weapons so long as they were "small." In fact, he added, "in legal theory Japan could have intercontinental ballistic missiles and atomic bombs."

Yet anti-war psychology in Japan runs deep. The lesson of the disaster of World War II remains strong. Millions of people visit Hiroshima and Nagasaki each year, which remain holy shrines against the evil of nuclear weapons. Japan associates war with horror, not valor. There is also a deep fear of things getting out of hand. The public realizes that Japan's political system has no brakes—once a policy has started, politicians and bureaucrats tend to carry it to incredible extremes. Former Singaporean Prime Minister Lee Kuan Yew once said, "To let an armed Japan participate in [peacekeeping operations] is like giving a chocolate filled with whiskey to an alcoholic." For years, leading politicians and pundits have called for revision of the constitution—yet nobody dares begin a process that might open Pandora's Box.

As Lee's comment shows, other Asian countries still view Japan with mistrust, and the Japanese recognize that for good neighborly relations they must never appear to wield military power. So Article 9 is a convenient disguise—the face Japan needs to show Asia. Meanwhile, it's easy, and cheap, to continue under America's "nuclear umbrella." So despite occasional squawks from Tokyo's hawks, Japan still sleeps in what Liberal Democratic Party stalwart Shizuka Kamei calls a "stupor of peace." Although they can hear the sound of North Korean drumbeats growing louder, most Japanese don't feel threatened. Life is comfortable. War and terror seem far away, an anachronism of little interest in today's Japan.

China Seeks Reform of North Korea

By David Shambaugh

This selection by David Shambaugh focuses on China's interests in North Korea and the Korean peninsula. Although China and North Korea historically have had close ties, North Korea, Shambaugh says, has been a longtime headache for China because of its provocative policies and behavior. For China, North Korea's 2002 announcement that it is pursuing nuclear weapons programs is only part of the larger problem of stabilizing the Korean peninsula. For this reason, halting North Korea's nuclear program is not the only or even the main focus of China's foreign policy.

Instead, China seeks to implement a comprehensive, long-term plan that will encourage North Korea to implement sustained economic reforms that will enable it to survive, stabilize, and ultimately integrate with South Korea. China's priorities, therefore, are to preserve the Kim Jong Il regime, to encourage regime reform, to maintain good relations with South Korea, to establish and maintain China's influence over the Korean peninsula, to slowly integrate North and South Korea, and, lastly, to encourage responsible North Korean behavior on security and military issues, including its nuclear weapons program. In the current crisis, therefore, China will likely seek a solution in which North Korea agrees to abandon its weapons of mass destruction in exchange for a plan that will encourage North Korean reform, integrate North and South Korea, and help normalize relations between the United States and North Korea. David Shambaugh is a professor of political science and international affairs and director of the China Policy Program at the Elliott School of International Affairs at George Washington University.

David Shambaugh, "China and the Korean Peninsula: Playing for the Long Term," *Washington Quarterly*, vol. 26, Spring 2003, pp. 43–56. Copyright © 2003 by The Center for Strategic and International Studies and the Massachusetts Institute of Technology. Reproduced by permission.

The unfolding international crisis concerning North Korea's nuclear weapons program has focused global attention on China's relations with its rogue neighbor. President George W. Bush and other world leaders have personally sought the Chinese government's influence and pressure on Pyongyang [the capital of North Korea], only to be given the nebulous reassurance that China seeks a nonnuclear Korean peninsula and that the problem must be solved peacefully. China's position is indeed central to resolving the crisis, but governments and analysts alike seem vexed to understand China's assessment of the situation, opaque positions, and apparent unwillingness to use its presumed leverage in tandem with others.

Chinese–North Korean Ties

Understanding China's calculus requires, at the outset, recognition that North Korea has been a long-standing headache for China. This is not the first time since the Chinese Communists came to power in 1949 that they find themselves in a difficult international quandary over the behavior of their erstwhile comrades in North Korea. Ever since Kim Il-sung's [the first leader of North Korea] forces invaded the South in 1950, China has repeatedly found its own national security interests affected and compromised by the provocative and confrontational policies pursued by the Kim dynasty and Pyongyang regime.

It is true that the Chinese Communist Party (CCP) and its North Korean counterpart have had long-standing ties and that the late Kim Il-sung was educated in China and was once a member of the CCP. It is also true that the two countries once had a formal alliance and mutually described their relationship as one of "lips and teeth." And it is true that China probably has better relations with the Democratic People's Republic of Korea (DPRK) [North Korea] than any other country on Earth. Despite these facts, however, the relationship between Beijing [the capital of China] and Pyongyang has been severely strained for many years, particularly since Kim Jung-il succeeded his father in 1995. Thus, from Beijing's perspective, the current crisis over North Korea's withdrawal from the 1994 Framework Agreement [an agreement signed by North Korea and the United States in which North Korea agreed to halt its nuclear weapons programs] and the Nuclear Non-Proliferation Treaty [an international treaty that seeks to stop the spread of nuclear weapons], as well as the DPRK's resumption of its nuclear weapons program, is only the latest chapter in a half-century of North Korean brinksmanship brought on by domestic desperation and disregard for its neighbors' interests and preferences.

Beijing considers the latest crisis an extremely serious situation, but permanently short-circuiting Pyongyang's nuclear ambitions is only a piece of a larger and more complicated puzzle for China. Despite China's strong and long-stated policy in favor of a nonnuclear Korean peninsula (both North and South), halting North Korea's nuclear program is not the ultimate end that China hopes to achieve. China's calculations, interests, and goals are more long term and more complicated. The United States and other involved nations must understand these perspectives and complexities if they are to effectively attain China's cooperation. . . .

China's Interests

China's policy calculus toward the DPRK—both in general and in the current crisis—involves a hierarchy of several interrelated interests:
1. DPRK regime survival;
2. DPRK regime reform;
3. maintaining and developing more comprehensively robust relations between China and South Korea;
4. establishing China's dominant external influence over the Korean peninsula (North and South);
5. integrating North and South, through economic and social means, leading to political unification over time; and
6. unprovocative and responsible North Korean behavior on security issues ranging from its nuclear weapons program to proliferation of other weapons of mass destruction (WMD) and their means of delivery to the deployments of DPRK conventional forces.

It is important to recognize that this hierarchy does not mean that China accepts the status quo on the peninsula. Although some analysts, particularly in the West, assume that China prefers the status quo to regime change, this is not in fact the case. China may favor the status quo over regime collapse, but China's preferred future for the DPRK is regime reform. China does not believe that the current situation on the peninsula or in the DPRK is stable or conducive either to regional stability or China's own national security, economic growth, or other national interests. For Beijing, enhancing stability is critical.

Consequently, China advocates a comprehensive policy package that would help set North Korea on the path to real reforms that involve the DPRK intensively with all its neighbors in Northeast Asia as well as the United States. For China, the issue is not simply whether the DPRK develops a nuclear weapons capacity or whether it will have a soft or hard landing from its current catastrophic state; the question is whether North Korea can embark on a sustained and comprehensive path of reform à la China. This is Beijing's positive vision for North Korea. (A less positive vision involves more incremental reform.) Understanding this long-term vision or goal is central to understanding the elements of China's strategy and tactics, or Beijing's "hierarchy of calculus."

Regime Survival

Most fundamentally, Beijing seeks to avoid the implosion or collapse of the DPRK regime and nation-state. Preventing collapse is Beijing's bottom line because collapse would have enormous tangible human and economic consequences for China, not to mention the intangible political impact of another failed Communist state. DPRK regime collapse could also potentially harm China's security.

China's aim to sustain the DPRK regime in no way suggests that Beijing likes the regime in Pyongyang. Quite to the contrary, Chinese officials and North Korea analysts in Beijing and Shanghai sometimes speak with disdain, despair, and heightened frustration when discussing the DPRK and China's relations with it. These critics deplore the sycophantic cult of personality surrounding the Kim dynasty, the Stalinist security state, the command economy, the poverty of the populace, the use of scarce resources for military purposes, the mass mobilization techniques of the regime, the autarkic paranoia about the world beyond its borders, and so forth. China's Korea analysts draw explicit parallels to Maoist China [a period of Chinese history in which Chairman Mao instituted economic reforms] (particularly during the Great Leap Forward [economic programs geared towards reforming China's economy]) and argue that North Korea's only viable option to avoid national suicide is to follow China's reformist example. They also recall anecdotal accounts of North Korean condescension toward visiting Chinese officials and confrontations with them.

As part of its regime survival strategy, Beijing believes that it must deal with the DPRK government and extends it aid in the form of foodstuffs and energy supplies to alleviate public suffering in North Korea. The exact amounts of this aid are not known, but estimates are in the range of 1 million tons of wheat and rice and 500,000 tons of heavy-fuel oil per annum since 1994. This estimate accounts for 70–90 percent of North Korea's fuel imports (and nearly 100 percent since the cutoff of U.S. heavy-fuel oil in December 2002) and about one-third of the DPRK's total food imports. Trade between the two countries, while minimal (amounting to $740 million in 2001 and approximately one-quarter of the DPRK's entire foreign trade), does supply needed consumer durables, energy supplies, and transport infrastructure. For a nation with negative economic growth, a paltry per capita income of $714, stagnant industrial production, an agricultural wasteland, and teetering on the verge of famine, China's aid and trade has been keeping the North Korean economy from total ruin and human calamity. . . .

Another irritating issue in the relationship has been cross-border migration, which has received international attention over the past year as North Korean migrants have made brazen attempts to enter diplomatic compounds in China to seek diplomatic asylum in South Korea or other countries. The refugee influx into China peaked in 2000 at approximately 200,000 by one estimate but has fallen to 100,000 or fewer since the Chinese government began a crackdown and forced repatriation in 2001. . . .

Prior to March 2001, when the crackdown began, those migrants who were apprehended were returned to North Korea, but most (even multiple offenders) were simply subjected to a 30-day reeducation program rather than harsh treatment. Since then, however, there is substantial evidence of a stricter Chinese policy aimed at apprehending and returning the migrants to North Korea, who often "meet execution, prison, torture, and detention in labor camps.". . .

On balance, China has been a critical actor in keeping the North Korean regime afloat and the North Korean population from a full-fledged and catastrophic famine. The Chinese government calculates that it is in its national interests to do so—both because a regime implosion would put a far heavier burden on China and because doing so is a half-step toward China's preferred strategy: real reform in North Korea.

Regime Reform

Since the early 1990s, Beijing has probably been the strongest external advocate of extensive economic and social reform to North Korea's autarkic *juche* policy [a policy of self-reliance implemented by its leader, Kim Il Sung]. China calculates that, if managed carefully, reforms do not necessarily being about the collapse of Communist regimes, as was the case in the USSR and Eastern Europe, but can strengthen the ruling party's base of support.

Kim Jong-il may be listening. He has visited China at least three times since May 2000 and may have made other secret visits. He has been shown the Zhongguancun computer district in Beijing, the skyscrapers and shopping centers of Shanghai, and export industries in Shenzhen. He has also received extensive briefings from Chinese officials and economists and has reportedly demonstrated a relatively sophisticated knowledge of various matters and asked astute questions.

Further exchanges to explore reforms have taken place at lower levels between the CCP's International Liaison Department (ILD) and its counterpart in the Korean Workers Party. (The ILD's annual almanac lists exchanges of between one and two dozen delegations annually in recent years.) Of course, the most noteworthy sign of Pyongyang's move down the Chinese reform path was the establishment of the Sinuiju Special Administrative Region near the Chinese border and the appointment of China's wealthiest businessman, Yang Bin, as the "governor" of the region. Before Yang Bin could take up his appointment, however, Chinese security officials arrested him on charges of tax fraud and other unspecified economic crimes.

While advocating economic and social (and implicitly political) reform, China realizes that reform in North Korea is a gamble—one that could easily exacerbate many of North Korea's dilemmas. Nevertheless, Beijing believes that pursuing reform is the best option and one in which China would play a significant economic role.

Relations with South Korea

The third element of China's policy calculus is deepening already robust ties with South Korea—both in their own right today as well as in anticipation of eventual unification of the two Koreas. Over the past decade, the relationship between China and the Republic of Korea (ROK) [South Korea] has completely transformed; it is now one of the strongest in the East Asian region. A kind of "China fever" has swept across South Korea, or at least the business community.

In 2001, China became South Korea's largest trading partner, surpassing the United States; South Korea is China's third-largest trade partner. Two-way trade in 2001 was approximately $40 billion and probably grew by 30 percent in 2002. The ROK is now the fifth-largest foreign investor in China, investing $830 million in 2001 and a projected $1 billion in 2002, and more than 8,000 South Korean companies now operate in China and employ hundreds of thousands of Chinese workers (particularly in the rust belt in the northeastern part of the country, where the Chinese government is trying to restructure and retool traditional heavy industries). South Korean firms are also very active in developing China's border region adjacent to North Korea. A dense network of transport links connecting the ROK with northeastern China and the Shandong peninsula facilitates the movement of goods, capital, and people. . . .

This relationship has become extremely important to Beijing as well as to Seoul, and the People's Republic of China (PRC) is not about to sacrifice it to placate Pyongyang in any way. (Needless to say, the PRC-ROK relationship now dwarfs PRC-DPRK relations.) Indeed, China's robust relations with South Korea act as a form of leverage with North Korea.

China's strategy for building ties with the South is born not only of economic motives but also of strategic calculations. Since the rapprochement more than a decade ago, Beijing has realized that it would have little leverage in shaping the eventual outcome of the divided Korean peninsula if it did not enjoy strong ties with South Korea. Such ties would also serve to offset any potential threat from the U.S.-ROK alliance and from U.S. forces on the peninsula. A close relationship would also serve to undercut or offset Japanese attempts to gain a stronger foothold on the peninsula. Beijing's strategy has been a net success, but both sides have reaped the benefits.

Beijing and Seoul consult with and support each other about strategy toward the DPRK. Both governments favor engagement with the North, a reformist North Korea, and eventual peaceful unification. The PRC and the ROK both oppose a punitive approach based on sanctions, and neither seems to endorse the Bush administration's policy of tailored containment. Both governments strongly oppose Pyongyang's WMD development, withdrawal from the Agreed Framework and the International Atomic Energy Agency (IAEA) safeguards program, and otherwise belligerent behavior. When ROK president Kim Dae-jung paid a state visit to Beijing in November 2002 to commemorate the tenth anniversary of the establishment of diplomatic relations, both sides reiterated the desire to maintain the Agreed Framework and to keep the peninsula free of nuclear weapons and other WMD.

In sum, China's entire approach to South Korea over the past decade has been motivated by four main factors: as a hedge against regime collapse in the North and/or potential unification of North and South Korea; as an astute economic investment; as a key component of its proactive peripheral diplomacy; and as a strategic ploy to gain long-term influence over the Korean peninsula.

Dominant External Influence

Although never publicly articulated, China tends to view the Korean peninsula as its natural sphere of influence—much as the United States views Latin America and Russia views Central Asia (and previously viewed the Baltic states and eastern Europe). Over the long term, geography will determine a great deal of the balance of power in Northeast Asia. China's proximity and growing interdependence will become, China hopes, the determining factor in the strategic orientation of both Korean states. This does not necessarily mean that China is looking to establish a new form of tributary vassal state (such as the one it maintained for several centuries), nor will it necessarily evolve into an asymmetrical patron-client relationship. The relationship will be deferential, however, and will likely mean that China will become more important to the Koreas than Japan, Russia, or the United States. At least, that is China's strategic calculus.

The outlines of this reconfigured relationship between China and the Koreas are already evident in the manner in which Seoul and Beijing now deal with each other. Not only is the relationship fully institutionalized, but both governments defer to each other's preferences (which are nearly identical when it comes to policy and strategy toward North Korea). Furthermore, China has been able to exploit South Korea's antipathy toward Japan to its advantage.

Any consideration of a dominant Chinese influence on the Korean peninsula must include the role of the United States and the presence of U.S. forces. How will China react to the alliance between the United States and the ROK and to U.S. military forces stationed on the peninsula following (presumptive) unification? Personal discussions with civilian analysts, Foreign Ministry officials, and military officers in China suggest that China's strong preference is that U.S. military involvement would no longer be an issue following unification and that the alliance would be naturally dissolved and troops withdrawn. . . .

Phased Integration of North and South Korea

Concomitant with China's aversion to the DPRK's sudden implosion is its opposition to a hasty integration of North and South Korea. Chinese analysts estimate that rapid unification would inevitably be both unmanageable and disruptive, making the burdens of German unification pale in comparison. A substantial part of the human, financial, energy, and environmental costs would ultimately fall on China.

Beijing prefers to pursue a gradual, phased integration, which will eventually lead to formal unification. A German model . . . is deemed the best way to proceed. This would involve a phased program of gradually increasing family, cultural, social, professional, and sports exchanges; direct transport links including rail links across the demilitarized zone (DMZ); commercial interchange, investment, and aid; intergovernmental exchanges; and a series of military confidence-building measures (CBMs) on both sides of the DMZ (one interesting model for these might be the CBMs that China and the Central Asian republics negotiated in the mid-1990s through the Shanghai Cooperation Organization). Once in place over several years, these various interactive measures would build the trust and confidence the two sides need to move toward discussions about formal political unification.

A More Responsible North Korea

The last of China's goals is somehow to persuade Pyongyang to halt its roguish behavior when it comes to weapons proliferation as well as its WMD development. North Korea's conventional military deployments are also a concern, but they are secondary to issues of nuclear proliferation and WMD development. To this end, China advocates a complete return to the Agreed Framework.

Although containing North Korea's nuclear program is a high Chinese priority, it is not by any means the first issue on Beijing's agenda. China sees these issues as part and parcel of the broader set of policy goals outlined above. There certainly exists exigency at present, and it must be addressed, but China's longer-term vision for North Korea goes well beyond WMD issues.

China's Role in Resolving the Current Crisis

Beijing's basic approach to the current crisis is to seek a package deal, concluded multilaterally, which trades North Korea's abandonment of WMD for a clear road map that will:
- set North Korea on the path to real reform,
- initiate a phased integration of North and South Korea, and
- help normalize relations between the United States and the DPRK.

Chances range from very doubtful to nil that Beijing will go along with Washington's new strategy of tailored containment or participate in a collective, sanctions-based punitive policy toward Pyongyang. This is simply not the way China prefers to deal with the problem. Ever since the 1994 crisis, China has been very clear that it firmly believes that a strategy of coercion and isolation not only will be counterproductive to gaining Pyongyang's cooperation but also is likely to prompt the North Korean regime to take desperate and potentially catastrophic actions.

The obsessive and singular focus on the issue of a nuclear buildup misses the broader environment that China wishes to foster on the Korean peninsula. At a minimum, from China's perspective—as clearly articulated by Chinese president Jiang Zemin and Russian president Vladimir Putin at their December 2002 summit meeting—the nuclear issue must be linked to "normalization" of U.S. relations with the DPRK. (In this context, at least, "normalization" does not necessarily imply diplomatic recognition; rather, it implies the kind of Liaison Office arrangement that the United States and China had between 1972 and 1979.) Beijing's bottom line is that there must be a package deal linked to a range of initiatives to help alleviate North Korea's chronic economic and social crises and to bring the DPRK into the international community.

Moreover, despite the strains in relations between Beijing and

Pyongyang, China is simply not going to allow North Korea to implode. The Chinese government will do whatever it can to alleviate human suffering and to keep the North Korean regime on life support. If worst came to worst, however, and the regime did peacefully collapse, Beijing believes that it holds a very strong hand in exercising its influence over a unified Korea.

China's current close relations with Russia also strengthen Beijing's influence. The solidarity on the North Korea issue that Jiang and Putin demonstrated at their December 2002 Beijing summit has sent a strong signal that the two governments do not wish to pursue a coercive and confrontational policy toward Pyongyang in an effort to resolve the current nuclear crisis. Even though the call to return to the Agreed Framework is probably unrealistic, the two leaders clearly signaled a preference for a multilateral and comprehensive solution to the nuclear problem.

China's Influence on U.S. Policy

Although some U.S. China analysts believe that the current crisis offers China a real opportunity to prove its credentials as a responsible power by siding with the Bush administration's tough approach to North Korea, it's actually the other way around. China seems to have the well-reasoned position based on a long-term perspective and road map for the Korean peninsula. Most importantly, China's position coincides with that of the other major powers and involved parties (South Korea, Russia, Japan, and the European Union). It is the United States that has struggled to find its footing on policy toward North Korea since the Bush administration took office in January 2001. The issue is not so much that Beijing should exercise its presumed influence or leverage over Pyongyang, as China does not have a great deal of influence in the first place and, in any event, does not choose to exercise it in an overtly coercive manner. China has constructively offered to host direct U.S.-DPRK talks in which Beijing could play an important facilitating role.

The Bush administration is still trying to satisfy its own conflicting impulses. On one hand, it is inclined to play hardball with the hardline North Korean regime; on the other hand, the administration recognizes that only a multilateral and comprehensive approach will solve the problem. Only time will tell whether the Bush administration's dual approach will work or whether the United States will have to join China, Russia, South Korea, Japan, the EU, and other actors in recognizing that only a comprehensive solution that starts by acknowledging that a reforming and outwardly engaged DPRK is the ultimate solution to the problem.

CHRONOLOGY

2000 B.C.
A culture develops in the area of Korea that emphasizes agriculture and a clan social structure, but it is not clear that Koreans were descended from these people.

1100–108 B.C.
The state of Old Choson rules on the Korean peninsula.

108 B.C. – A.D. 313
The Han Chinese rule on the Korean peninsula.

A.D. 300s
The three kingdoms develop on the Korean peninsula (Paekche, Koguryo, and Silla).

668
After years of conflict among the three kingdoms, the kingdom of Silla emerges victorious, defeating the other kingdoms. This begins a thirteen-hundred-year period of unification on the Korean peninsula.

936–1392
The Koryo dynasty rules Korea.

1392–1910
The Choson or Yi dynasty rules Korea.

1895
In the Sino-Japanese Treaty of Shimonoseki, China recognizes the independence of Korea, giving Japan greater influence over the area.

1905
Japan wins the Russo-Japanese War, and Russia acknowledges Japan's rights to Korea, opening the way for Japanese annexation.

1910
Japan officially annexes Korea, beginning a period of four decades of brutality and repression for Koreans as a Japanese colony.

1919
Mass protests of Japan's colonization of Korea occur throughout Korea (March First Movement).

1931–1941
Japan is successful in a series of military conquests that eventually lead Japan into World War II, aligned with Germany and Italy.

1941
The Japanese attack Pearl Harbor, Hawaii, bringing the United States into World War II.

1945
Japan surrenders to the Allies, ending World War II. Korea is freed from Japanese colonialism but is occupied by Russia in the north and the United States in the south. Russia and the United States propose a five-year trusteeship for Korea.

1945–1947
Russia and the United States attempt but fail to negotiate the terms of the trusteeship and provisional government.

1947
The United Nations (UN) votes to sponsor elections in Korea, over Russian objections.

1948
Russia prohibits the UN representatives from entering the north, so the United Nations holds elections in the south. In August the Republic of Korea (ROK) is created in South Korea, and Syngman Rhee is elected as its first president.

On September 9, the Democratic People's Republic of Korea (DPRK) is proclaimed in North Korea, and Kim Il Sung, backed by the Soviet Union, is chosen to become its leader. North Korea begins to make guerrilla raids on South Korea. At the end of 1948, the Soviets withdraw their troops from North Korea.

1950
The Korean War begins when North Korean troops invade South Korea on June 25, with backing from Communist Soviet Union. U.S. president Harry S. Truman sends American troops to defend South Korea. The United Nations adopts a resolution demanding that

North Korea retreat and asking member states to help South Korea.

In September U.S. general Douglas MacArthur leads allied troops in a military campaign that lands in the port of Inch'ŏn, pushes North Korean troops northward, and retakes South Korea. MacArthur then captures P'yŏngyang in North Korea and pushes northward toward the Chinese border.

In November China sends troops to aid North Korea, and they press the allied troops back into South Korea, capturing Seoul.

1951

In March the allied troops retake Seoul.

1951–1953

Armistice talks begin in July 1951, but the war continues until July 27, 1953.

1953

The Korean War ends with an armistice agreement on July 27, 1953, and a 2.5-mile-wide demilitarized zone (DMZ) is created just north of the thirty-eighth parallel, separating North and South Korea. No formal peace treaty is signed, and North and South Korea remain technically at war.

1954

Negotiations fail on a peace treaty, or any plan for reuniting North and South Korea. The United States and South Korea sign a Mutual Defense Treaty, providing for U.S. troops to remain in South Korea.

1961

North Korea signs military assistance treaties with China and the Soviet Union.

1968

North Korea seizes the USS *Pueblo*, a U.S. intelligence ship, in the Sea of Japan.

North Korean commando troops attack Seoul, and there are clashes between North and South Korea at the DMZ.

1969

North Korea downs a U.S. reconnaissance plane.

1972
North Korea approves a new constitution, making Kim Il Sung president as well as prime minister.

1974
A tunnel dug by North Korea under the DMZ is discovered, and a second tunnel is discovered in February 1975.
North Korea attempts to assassinate South Korean president Park Chung Hee.

1977
The United States plans a gradual withdrawal of troops from South Korea.

1980
Kim Jong Il, Kim Il Sung's son, is given senior posts in the Politburo, the Military Commission, and the Party Secretariat and is openly proclaimed as Kim Il Sung's successor.

1981
U.S. president Ronald Reagan ends troop withdrawals from South Korea.

1983
In October North Korean agents attempt to assassinate South Korean president Chun Doo Hwan with a bomb. The president is not harmed, but the bomb kills seventeen members of his entourage.

1985
North Korea signs the Nuclear Non-Proliferation Treaty but does not agree to inspections by the International Atomic Energy Agency.

1986
The United States detects evidence that North Korea is developing nuclear weapons.

1987
In November agents of North Korea sabotage a Korean Airlines plane, killing all 115 passengers.

1988
In January the United States places North Korea on its list of states supporting international terrorism. North Korea also is under a

U.S. embargo on trade and financial transactions under the Trading with the Enemy Act.

The Seoul Olympics are held in South Korea from September 17 through October 2.

Beginning in December, the United States conducts talks with North Korea regarding missiles and other topics.

1990

On Kim Il Sung's seventy-eighth birthday, massive demonstrations are held in North Korea in support of his regime. He is reelected president in 1991.

1991

The Soviet Union, one of North Korea's most important allies and economic supporters, collapses, leading to increasingly serious economic problems in North Korea.

1992

In January North Korea signs an implementing agreement for the Nuclear Non-Proliferation Treaty agreeing to allow inspections of its nuclear facilities, after six years of stonewalling. Between June 1992 and February 1993, North Korea permits the International Atomic Energy Agency (IAEA) to conduct six inspections of the country's seven declared nuclear facilities.

1993

On March 12 North Korea withdraws from the Nuclear Non-Proliferation Treaty and refuses to allow inspections, causing a serious crisis with the United States. In May 1993 the UN Security Council passes a resolution urging North Korea to cooperate with the IAEA and implement the treaty. The United States begins talks with North Korea aimed at resolving the nuclear issue.

1994

In June former U.S. president Jimmy Carter holds talks with Kim Il Sung, defusing a growing crisis over North Korea's nuclear capabilities.

On July 7 North Korea announces the death of Kim Il Sung at age eighty-two. He is succeeded by his son, Kim Jong Il.

Negotiations with the United States resume after the death of Kim Il Sung, and on October 21 North Korea and the United States negotiate and sign the Framework Agreement, in which North Korea promises to halt its development of nuclear weapons in return for aid in building civilian nuclear reactors and temporary oil supplies.

1995
Floods afflict North Korea, causing agricultural losses and food shortages and requiring the country to appeal for foreign aid. Japan and South Korea donate food.

1996
Serious food shortages continue in North Korea, reaching famine proportions.

On April 16 the United States and South Korea propose four-party peace talks among the two Koreas, the United States, and China aimed at replacing the 1953 armistice agreement with a permanent peace treaty. Thereafter, a series of meetings are held between August 1997 and August 1999, but the parties are unable to agree on an agenda for the talks. The talks stall.

1997
Kim Jong Il is named secretary of the Korean Workers' Party.

1998
The food shortages become critical because of a drought that follows the earlier floods. The government of North Korea imposes food rationing.

President Kim Dae Jung of South Korea announces his "Sunshine Policy," which seeks to improve relations with North Korea through negotiation and cooperation.

On August 31 North Korea launches a multistage rocket over Japan. Japan imposes sanctions on North Korea. The launch celebrates Kim Jong Il's consolidation of power in North Korea and his taking of the title of National Defense Commission chairman. Kim Il Sung is to be the eternal president of the country, even in death. North Korea openly admits that it exports missiles to a number of countries and suggests that if the United States wishes to stop the exports, it should lift its economic embargo on North Korea and compensate North Korea for the losses that would be caused by discontinuing missile exports.

1999
In September the United States agrees to lift economic sanctions against North Korea, and North Korea announces an end to missile testing. Despite this announcement, however, North Korea

continues to develop long-range nuclear-capable missiles and continues to export missile technology.

Tensions between North and South Korea increase due to the sinking of a North Korean ship and the arrest by North Korea of a South Korean tourist accused of spying.

2000–2001

Between June 13 and 15, North Korean leader Kim Jong Il and South Korean president Kim Dae Jong meet for a summit in P'yŏngyang and sign a joint declaration pledging to work for reunification. Also in June, North Korea agrees to extend its ban on missile testing, and the United States thereafter relaxes economic sanctions on North Korea.

Between August 15 and 18, North and South Korea permit a reunion of 1,170 persons for the first time since they were separated by the Korean War. A second family reunion takes place for 1,220 persons between November 30 and December 2, 2000, and a third for 1,240 persons between February 16 and 18, 2001. Other attempts at economic cooperation begin, including reconnection of a railway between the north and south, development of an industrial complex by the Hyundai Group in North Korea, a flood prevention project for the Imjin River in North Korea, and other economic agreements. Social and cultural exchanges also begin between the two countries.

U.S. secretary of state Madeleine Albright visits North Korea, but no official agreement is reached on missile testing.

U.S. president George W. Bush is elected in November.

2001

In January the new U.S. Bush administration suspends diplomatic relations with North Korea and orders a review of American policy toward the country. In June 2001 the United States proposes negotiations on nuclear and conventional weapons issues as well as North Korea's continued military presence at the DMZ, but North Korea rejects the proposal.

Official talks between North and South Korea as part of the 2000 summit stall, and peace initiatives, such as the family reunions and other joint efforts, end. In South Korea, public support for South Korea's Sunshine Policy toward North Korea dissipates.

2002

On January 29 President Bush announces in his State of the Union address that North Korea is part of an "axis of evil" (along with Iraq and Iran) that threatens the world with the development of weapons of mass destruction.

Talks begin between the United States and North Korea, and on October 4 North Korea announces that it is developing nuclear weapons in violation of the 1994 Framework Agreement with the United States. North Korea demands bilateral talks with the United States and a nonaggression treaty to end the crisis.

Later in October, representatives of North and South Korea meet for the first time since talks stalled in 2001.

In November the United States and its allies cut off fuel oil promised to North Korea. Thereafter, in November and December, North Korea escalates the nuclear crisis by removing surveillance cameras from its nuclear facility, moving fuel rods to a storage site near its nuclear reactor and reprocessing plant, threatening to reopen its reprocessing plant, and ordering UN inspectors to leave the country.

In December South Korea votes for a successor to President Kim Dae Jung, who pursued a Sunshine Policy of reconciliation toward North Korea. On December 19 Roh Moo Hyun, who favors continued engagement with North Korea, is elected president of South Korea.

2003

On January 10 North Korea says it is pulling out of the Nuclear Non-Proliferation Treaty. It also hints that it might drop its moratorium on missile tests.

On January 14 the United States proposes that some combination of economic, food, and energy aid might be considered in combination with security guarantees, but only if North Korea first agrees to give up its nuclear arms program. North Korea rejects the offer, refusing to accept disarmament as a condition for talks. Thereafter, the United States pushes for multinational talks involving China, Japan, and South Korea.

On January 30 U.S. surveillance shows North Korean trucks apparently moving spent nuclear fuel rods, possibly to be reprocessed into weaponry.

On February 3 the United States puts twenty-four long-range bombers on alert for possible deployment within range of North Korea.

On February 5, North Korea announces that it has reactivated its nuclear facilities but promises that its nuclear activity will be limited to peaceful purposes such as the production of electricity.

On February 6 North Korea warns of "total war" if the United States dares to attack its nuclear complex. The United States responds, warning North Korea against trying to take advantage of the U.S. focus on Iraq, saying it will maintain a robust military deterrent in the region even as it seeks a diplomatic solution to the nuclear crisis.

On February 16 the United States says it is developing plans for sanctions against North Korea that will include halting its weapons shipments and cutting off money sent there by Koreans living in Japan.

On February 18 North Korea threatens to abandon its commitment to the 1953 Korean War armistice if the United States moves to impose penalties like a naval blockade.

On February 20 a North Korean fighter plane flies into South Korean airspace until it is pursued by South Korean jets and is forced to return to North Korean territory.

On February 24 North Korea test fires a short-range cruise missile into the Sea of Japan.

On February 25 the new South Korean president, Roh Moo Hyun, takes office.

On February 27 North Korea restarts a reactor in its nuclear facilities.

On March 2 North Korean fighter jets intercept an unarmed U.S. spy plane on a surveillance mission.

On March 10 North Korea test fires a medium-range antiship missile over the Sea of Japan.

On April 16 North Korea, the United States, and China agree to hold talks.

FOR FURTHER RESEARCH

Books

Tsuneo Akaha, *The Future of North Korea.* New York: Routledge, 2002.

Tai Sung An, *North Korea: A Political Handbook.* Wilmington, DE: Scholarly Resources, 1983.

D. Ellsworth Blanc, ed., *North Korea, Pariah?* Huntington, NY: Novinka Books, 2001.

James Brady, *The Coldest War: A Memoir of Korea.* New York: Thomas Dunne Books, 1990.

Adrian Buzo, *The Making of Modern Korea.* New York: Routledge, 2002.

Young Back Choi, ed., *Perspectives on Korean Unification and Economic Integration.* Cheltenham, UK: Edward Elgar, 2001.

Bruce Cumings, *Korea's Place in the Sun.* New York: W.W. Norton, 1997.

Chuck Downs, *Over the Line, North Korea's Negotiating Strategy.* Washington, DC: AIE, 1999.

Nicholas Eberstadt and Richard J. Ellings, eds., *Korea's Future and the Great Powers.* Seattle: National Bureau of Asian Research in association with the University of Washington Press, 2001.

Alexandra Kura, *Rogue Countries: Background and Current Issues.* Huntington, NY: Nova Science, 2001.

Chong-Sik Lee and Se-Hee Yoo, eds., *North Korea in Transition.* Berkeley, CA: Institute of East Asian Studies, University of California at Berkeley, 1991.

Donald Stone Macdonald, *The Koreans: Contemporary Politics and Society.* Boulder, CO: Westview, 1996.

Han S. Park, *North Korea: The Politics of Unconventional Wisdom.* Boulder, CO: Lynne Rienner, 2002.

Stanley Sandler, *The Korean War: No Victors, No Vanquished.* Lexington: University Press of Kentucky, 1999.

Han Woo-keun, *The History of Korea.* Seoul: Eul-Yoo, 1970.

Periodicals

Yinhay Ahn, "North Korea in 2001: At a Crossroads," *Asian Survey,* January/February 2002.

David Albright and Holly Higgins, "North Korea: It's Taking Too Long: Inspections in North Korea Are Tied to the Reactor Deal, Which Is Far Behind Schedule," *Bulletin of the Atomic Scientists,* January/February 2002.

Bulletin of the Atomic Scientists, "Letter from Pyongyang," July/August 2002.

Business Week, "The Two Koreas: What's Behind a Break in the Ice," April 15, 2002.

Victor D. Cha, "North Korea's Weapons of Mass Destruction: Badges, Shields, or Swords?" *Political Science Quarterly,* Summer 2002.

Stan Crock, "Why Bush Must Talk to Pyongyang," *Business Week Online,* October 25, 2002.

Bruce Cumings, "Endgame in Korea," *Nation,* November 18, 2002.

———, "Summitry in Pyongyang," *Nation,* July 10, 2000.

Hugh Deane, "Korea, China, and the United States: A Look Back," *Monthly Review,* February 1995.

Michael Duffy and Nancy Gibbs, "When Evil Is Everywhere: Has Bush Been Right All Along, or Is His World View Part of the Problem?" *Time,* October 28, 2002.

Economist, "Getting the Genie Back into the Bottle; North Korea's Nuclear Programme," October 26, 2002.

———, "Stitch by Stitch to a Different World; Free-Market Stirrings in North Korea," July 27, 2002.

Kristen Eichensehr, "Broken Promises," *Harvard International Review,* Fall 2001.

Thomas H. Henrikson, "The Rise and Decline of Rogue States," *Vital Speeches,* March 1, 2001.

Donald Kirk, "Opportunity Time for the Koreas," *New Leader*, September/October 2000.

Tae-Hwan Kwak and Seung-Ho Joo, "The Korean Peace Process: Problems and Prospects After the Summit," *World Affairs*, Fall 2002.

Robert A. Manning, "The Enigma of the North," *Wilson Quarterly*, Summer 1999.

National Review, "North Korea: Proliferation," November 11, 2002.

Don Oberdorfer, "Better Start Talking—and Fast," *Time*, January 13, 2003.

Thomas Omestad and Mark Mazzetti, "North Korea Breaks a No-Nukes Deal," *U.S. News & World Report*, October 28, 2002.

Phillip Park, "The Future of the Democratic People's Republic of Korea," *Journal of Contemporary Asia*, March 2001.

Progressive, "Axis to Grind," March 2002.

Scott Snyder, "North Korea's Challenge of Regime Survival: Internal Problems and Implications for the Future," *Pacific Affairs*, Winter 2000.

Jonathan Watts, "Balancing the 'Axis of Evil' in Northeast Asia," *Lancet*, September 7, 2002.

Websites

Asian Info, www.asianinfo.org. This website is dedicated to introducing Asian culture, traditions, and general information to the world.

Federation of American Scientists, www.fas.org. This is the website for a nonprofit organization founded in 1945 by members of the Manhattan Project, creators of the atom bomb. Its focus is the implications of nuclear power and weaponry for the future of humankind, and it contains information about North Korea's nuclear program.

Korean News Service, www.kcna.co.jp. This is the website for the Korean Central News Agency, a state-run agency of the Democratic People's Republic of Korea (DPRK). It speaks for the Workers' Party of Korea and the DPRK government.

Korea Web Weekly, www.kimsoft.com. This is a website on all things

Korean. It includes information on history, culture, economy, politics, and military.

U.S. Central Intelligence Agency (CIA), *The World Factbook 2002, North Korea*, ww.cia.gov. This is a U.S. government website for the CIA, providing geographical, political, economic, and other information on the country of North Korea as well as reports and speeches about recent political issues.

INDEX

American Enterprise Institute, 74
arms dealing, 13, 15, 50–51, 55–56, 86, 96
Arnold, Archibald V., 25
Arrigoni, Guy R., 32

ballistic missiles, 13, 55–56
Becker, Jasper, 43
Bennett, Bruce, 90
biological weapons. *See* weapons of mass destruction
Biological Weapons Convention, 53
Bok Ku Lee, 85
Bolton, John, 50
Brzezinski, Zbigniew, 74
Buddhist Sharing Movement, 42
Bush, George W.
 administration of, North Korea policies and, 110
 on "axis of evil," 9, 45, 48–49
 on dialogue between United States and North Korea, 56, 78
 initial position of, on North Korea, 14
 "nuclear blackmail" labeling by, 78
 on terrorist-sponsoring nations, 9, 14, 45–49
 on U.S. alliance with South Korea, 51
 on war on terrorism, 14

Central Intelligence Agency (CIA), 64
Cha, Victor, 95
chemical weapons. *See* weapons of mass destruction
Chemical Weapons Convention, 53
China
 complexity of relations with North Korea, 42, 66, 102, 103–105, 109–10
 as deterrent to Asian nuclear crisis, 94, 96
 direct negotiation between United States and North Korea and, 75, 77, 109, 110
 economic policies of, 11, 106–107
 North Korea policies of, 66, 67, 102, 103–105, 108–109, 110
 refugee problems in, 66, 105
 regional ambitions of, 103–104, 107–108, 109–10
 South Korea and, 106–108
 unification of Koreas and, 108
Choson dynasty, 18
Chun Doo Hwan, 11
Chung Ju Yung, 42
Chung Min Lee, 73
Chun Hoo Dwan, 32, 33
Cold War, 21, 25, 26–31
communism, 19–20, 26
 see also China; North Korea; Russia
Council on Foreign Relations, 74
Cumings, Bruce G., 17

defectors, 88
demilitarization. *See* North Korea, stabilization program of
demilitarized zone (DMZ), 52
Democratic People's Republic of Korea (DPRK). *See* North Korea
Dobbs, Lou, 72
domino effect, 94–95
drought, 11, 13
Du Mars, Roger, 94

East Asian Nonproliferation

Program, 75
Eberstadt, Nicholas, 74
economic crisis, 13, 35, 37, 73
Einhorn, Robert, 96

famine, 13, 42–43
floods, 12, 35, 36
foreign aid, 36, 41–42
Framework Agreement (1994), 11, 56–59, 68, 69, 76, 79, 82–83

Galluci, Robert, 73

Hanawald, Jennifer, 94
Han Woo-keun, 21
Heginbotham, Eric, 74
highly enriched uranium (HEU). *See* weapons of mass destruction
Hodges, John R., 25, 27
hunger, 36, 37, 38
Hwang Jang Yop, 39

Imai, Ryukichi, 97
International Atomic Energy Agency (IAEA), 54–55, 56, 60, 69
isolation, 13, 63–64

Japan
 aid to North Korea and, 42
 normalization of relations with North Korea, 66, 80
 occupation of Korean peninsula by, 10, 17, 18–20, 22
 pacifist policy of, 98
 weapons of mass destruction and, 97, 98, 99–100
Jiang Zemin, 109–10
Joint North-South Denuclearization Agreement of 1992, 55
Joint Parallel, 52

Kelly, James, 62–63
Kerr, Alex, 98
Kim Il Sung
 attacks on South Korea under, 32–34
 on biological weapon production, 53
 dictatorship of, 26
 policies and strategies of, 11–12
 political party of, 28
 as resistance leader, 17, 20
Kim Jong Il
 ambiguity of, 60
 arms dealing and, 96
 China and, 105–106
 declining power of, 88
 on economic collapse, 38–40, 72
 militarism of, 13, 35, 40, 72
 terrorism and, 34
 unification of Koreas and, 92–93
Kim Ku, 20, 26
Kim Kyu-sik, 28
Kim Young Tak, 97
Korean Airlines terrorist incident, 32, 34
Korean peninsula
 Cold War effect upon, 21, 26–31
 contrast between North Korea and South Korea, 73, 92–93
 division of, 25–31
 foreign occupation and influence in, 9–11, 18–19, 21–31
 map of, 12
 nationalist resistance movements in, 19–20
 peace process between North Korea and South Korea, 15
 political resistance and leadership traditions of, 17, 18–20
 United Nations and, 29–31
Korean Peninsula Energy Development Organization (KEDO), 67
Korean War, 11, 30–31

Laney, James T., 57

MacArthur, Douglas, 26, 31
malnutrition, 35

Manchuria, 17, 20, 22
Mazzetti, Mark, 94
militarism, 35, 40, 81–82
missiles, 13, 14, 55–56

North Korea
  ambiguity of foreign policy regarding WMD in, 15, 54–56, 75, 76–77, 82–83
  as "axis of evil" component, 48, 55–56
  ballistic missiles and, 13, 73
  as characterized by policy disagreements, 80–81
  Chemical Weapons Convention and, 53
  Communist-bloc characteristics of, 9, 30
  economic crisis in, 43, 81–82
  founding of, 9
  isolation of, by other nations, 63–64
  juche policy of, 105
  leadership sources in, 20
  map of, 12, 61
  as miscalculating in recent foreign policies, 63
  as motivated by fear of U.S. security threats, 57, 62, 67, 68–71, 78
  as "nuclear blackmailer," 74
  oppression and hardships of people in, 11, 13, 65, 86, 87, 88
  planning attack on South Korea, 81
  stabilization program of, 57–58, 60, 66, 67
  terrorist activities of, 11, 32, 33–34
  U.S. negotiations and, 57, 60, 63, 65, 66–67, 77, 79–80
  as WMD producer and dealer, 53, 72, 73–74, 94–96
  see also arms dealing
Nuclear Non-Proliferation Treaty, 14, 60, 68, 70–71, 77, 95
nuclear weapons. *See* weapons of mass destruction

Oberdorfer, Don, 35
Omestad, Thomas, 94

Paek Nam Sun, 58
Page, Trevor, 36
Pak Hon-yong, 20
People's Republic of China. *See* China
Perry, William, 82
plutonium production, 76
Powell, Colin, 51, 52, 58
Putin, Vladimir, 109–10

RAND, 90
Republic of China. *See* Taiwan
Republic of Korea (ROK). *See* South Korea
Rhee, Syngman, 20, 26, 28, 29–30
Roh Moo Hyun, 96
Russia, 67, 75, 77, 109, 110

Saunders, Phillip C., 75
Shambaugh, David, 101
Shaplen, Jason T., 57
So Chae-p'il, 28
Song Young Dae, 39
South Korea
  defectors from North Korea and, 88
  economic strength of, 81
  map of, 12
  military modernization and training improvement in, 81
  North Korea as threat to, 90, 91–93
  Sunshine Policy of, 80, 86–90
  trade relationship with China, 106
  weapons of mass destruction and, 97
Soviet Union, 10–11, 37
stalemate, 58, 65
starvation, 38
Suh Dong Kwon, 37
Sunshine Policy, 80, 86–90

Syria, 55

Taiwan, 97
terrorism, 33–34
38th parallel, 52
Tilelli, John H., 40–41
trusteeship, 26–30

United Nations (UN)
　aid to North Korea from, 13
　Food and Agricultural
　　Organization, 36–37
　World Food Program, 36–37
United Nations Committee for the
　Unification and Rehabilitation of
　Korea (UNCURK), 29–30
United States
　advantage of, 57, 60, 65, 66–67
　ambiguity of North Korean
　　intentions and, 13, 83
　arguments against direct
　　negotiations with North Korea,
　　48–49, 76, 77, 86–88
　con, 75, 77, 83–84, 109, 110
　defectors from North Korea and,
　　88
　as enemy of and threat to North
　　Korea, 68–71
　foreign policy alternatives for
　　North Korea and, 74
　military attack on North Korean
　　WMD infrastructure, 83
　mistrust of North Korea by, 79
　mobilization by, of international
　　pressure against North Korea, 83
　multilateral two-stage solution and,
　　66–67
　North Korean willingness to
　　negotiate with, 59
　"nuclear blackmail" and, 75, 76
uranium-enrichment program, 77
　see also weapons of mass
　　destruction

war on terror, 14
weapons of mass destruction
　(WMD)
　history of development by North
　　Korea, 85–86
　as necessity for North Korea's
　　security, 78
　North Korean concealment of,
　　52–55
　as North Korean negotiating tool
　　for economic and security
　　concessions, 78–79
　North Korean production of, 13–15
　as strategic preparation for attack
　　on South Korea, 81
World War II, 22–26

Yo Un-hyong, 28